D1080149

# FIGHTER!

# FIGHTER!

## BILL GUNSTON

OBE FRAeS

PARRAGON

*Page one: This Spitfire LF.IXc was one of a batch of 2,190 built at the Vickers-Armstrongs factory at Castle Bromwich. Today we buy fighters in ones and twos!*

*Pages two and three: The all-wood de Havilland Mosquito was the most versatile aircraft of World War II. Very few of the 7,781 built still exist, and even fewer are airworthy. Tragically this example – unarmed dual-control trainer T.3 RR299 – crashed in 1996.*

This is a Parragon Book

© Parragon 1997
Reprinted 1998

Parragon
13 Whiteladies Road, Clifton,
Bristol BS8 1PB United Kingdom

Designed, produced and packaged by
Touchstone
Old Chapel Studio, Plain Road, Marden,
Tonbridge, Kent TN12 9LS
United Kingdom

Edited by Philip de Ste. Croix

ISBN 0-75252-608-1

Printed in Italy

**Photographic Credits:**
*(Abbreviations: r = right, l = left, c = centre, t = top, b = below)*
The publishers would like to thank the following for permission to reproduce their photographs:

**Philip Jarrett**
Pages 8-9, 9b, 10, 11b, 12l, 13r, 14, 15t, 16, 17b, 18, 19t, 19b, 20, 21t, 23t, 25l, 26-27, 27t, 30, 31t, 31b, 32, 33t, 35t, 35b, 36, 37t, 40, 41t, 41b, 42, 43b, 44, 46, 47t, 48, 49t, 50b, 54, 56, 58, 59t, 65t, 65b, 68, 69t, 69b, 71t, 74, 75t, 78, 94l.

**Jeremy Flack/Aviation Photographs International**
Pages 6, 7b, 9t, 15b, 24, 29t, 38, 43t, 52, 53t, 53b, 57t, 59b, 60, 61t, 61b, 62, 63b, 64, 67b, 70, 71b, 75, 79t, 80, 81t, 82l, 83t, 85t, 85b, 88, 89t, 89b, 90r, 91, 94r.

**John Dibbs/The Plane Picture Company**
Pages 1, 2-3, 7t, 11t, 12-13c, 17t, 21b, 22-23b, 25r, 27b, 28, 29b, 34-35, 39t, 39b, 45, 47b, 48-49c, 50t, 51, 55t, 55b, 57b, 76, 86, 87t.

**Philip de Ste. Croix**
Pages 33b (Department of Defense), 63t (Dassault/Aviaplans – François Robineau), 66 (Armée de l'Air), 67t (Saab Scania), 72 (Dassault/Aviaplans – François Robineau), 73t (SIRPA AIR), 73b (Dassault/Aviaplans – François Robineau), 77t (Lockheed Martin), 77b (Saab Scania), 81b (Grumman Corporation), 82-83 (McDonnell Douglas Corporation), 90r (McDonnell Douglas Corporation), 92 (Dassault/Aviaplans – François Robineau), 93t (Dassault/Aviaplans – François Robineau), 93b (British Aerospace plc), 95t (Boeing Defense & Space Group), 95b (Lockheed Martin).

**Bill Gunston**
Pages 69c (Mikoyan), 79b (Rolls-Royce), 84 (Mikoyan), 87b (Saab Scania).

**Philip J. Birtles**
Page 37b.

# CONTENTS

# INTRODUCTION

Aviation enthusiasts can't really blame themselves for the fact
that the aircraft that excite them most, and draw crowds to
airshows, are weapons of war called fighters.

Bombers also have their appeal, but there is something about the speed, agility and sheer 'sexiness' of the fighter that gives it a head start. Added to this is the fact that most are crewed not by a team but by one man – oops!, bearing in mind the Soviet girls of 'the Great Patriotic War' and not a few female fighter pilots of

today, by one *person*. Like the knights of old, they garb for the fray and then fight personal battles.

Thus, though there are a few 'ground attack' and even Jumbo Jet interactive videos, most of the electronic flying games of today put the player in the ejection seat of a fighter. In passing, it is fair to

*Below: Two of the greatest adversaries of World War II are today the best of friends. Supermarine Spitfire LF.XVIe RW382, in the markings of RAF No 604 Squadron, is seen here accompanied by Messerschmitt Bf 109G-2 'Black 6', which has British civil registration G-USTV, because to its pilots the 109G was a 'Gustav'.*

*Above: When is a fighter not a fighter? To anyone in the media this Jaguar attack bomber would be 'a fighter', and as it has two cannon and can carry air-to-air missiles it can certainly shoot down other aircraft. Here a Jaguar of RAF No 16 Squadron begins a loop whilst carrying drop tanks and an electronic countermeasures pod.*

*" Many boys may not have thought that superiority in aerial-dogfight games really would give them a head start were they to try it for real and join the air force."*

*Right: Lifted as well as propelled by its unique engine, the British Aerospace Sea Harrier is the only fighter in service anywhere in the world which does not need either an airfield or an aircraft carrier. Having performed brilliantly in the South Atlantic campaign in 1982, the Sea Harrier FRS.1 is now being replaced by the radar-equipped FRS.2. Here an FRS.1 is aiming its two 30mm guns at the photographer.*

comment that some of these games really do simulate the air-combat scenario very well, though perhaps without the terror, bone-crushing 'g-force' in manoeuvres and physical exertion which leaves the 'fighter jock' drained and soaked in perspiration! Many boys may not have thought that superiority in aerial-dogfight games really would give them a head start were they to try it for real and join the air force.

This book aims to give a broad overview of how fighters were conceived, and how their design has changed over the past 80 years. Though today's aircraft may appear to be utterly unlike those that fought the deadly duels of World War I, many of the basic laws are immutable, and cannot really change.

For example, every fighter has to have one or more engines. It is simple to give it more or bigger engines, but this will make it heavier and thus more sluggish in manoeuvres. It will also burn fuel more rapidly, so unless weight is increased even more by carrying much more fuel, the range (the distance it can fly) will be reduced.

Again, most fighters need to be agile, and beat the enemy in turning manoeuvres. This is again seemingly simple: you just make the wing(s) bigger. This also enables the aircraft to take off and land in a shorter distance, but a bigger wing makes the fighter slower. Likewise, the armament is a compromise. In World War II many fighters had four large shell-firing cannon, but some of the most successful aces preferred lighter armament, so that they could turn better than the enemy, relying on their superior marksmanship.

A few of the older aircraft pictured are accurate replicas. No high-quality colour photographs exist of the originals.

# THE DAWN OF AIR COMBAT

It is difficult for us today to comprehend the apparent
stupidity of military and civilian leaders in the period 1910-14.
They dismissed the idea of warfare in the air as nonsense.

A few went so far as to admit that aircraft might be useful in reconnaissance, flying over the battlefield and reporting the positions of enemy troops. It never occurred to anyone in authority that, if both sides did this, the aircraft might interfere with each other.

Among the general public there were visionaries who could see what might happen. They saw that a pilot could aim his entire aircraft at an enemy and then fire a machine gun fixed to fire straight ahead. This was easy to arrange with 'pusher' aircraft, with the propeller at the back.

But the fastest aeroplanes had tractor propellers, mounted on the front, so five inventors proposed arrangements to control the firing of a machine gun so that it did not damage a propeller just in front of the muzzle. Nobody in authority showed any interest.

Aircraft had fired guns and dropped small home-made bombs at airshows and even in actual wars in the period 1910-14. After World War I broke out in August 1914 it was soon apparent that soldiers would fire their rifles at any flying machine passing overhead. This led to painting on national markings, and to instruction in how to tell one type of aircraft from another. Before the year was out pilots and observers were arming themselves with rifles, machine guns, pistols and even shotguns!

On 5 October 1914 a French observer in a Voisin shot down a 'Hun' with a machine gun. Some thought this rather unsporting, and there was still no such thing as a fighter.

*Above: This replica Fokker E.III Eindecker flies in today's peaceful skies, but we can imagine the fear it inspired in Allied pilots in 1915. This was simply because this quite light and flimsy monoplane had the world's first really effective fighter armament.*

*Left: The Aircraft Manufacturing Co, at Hendon, delivered 400 D.H.2 fighters to the Royal Flying Corps. Putting the propeller behind the pilot was the easy way to fit a machine gun to fire ahead (the gun is not fitted to this example). Once pilots mastered the idea of aiming the whole aircraft, the D.H.2 did well.*

*Below: The French Morane-Saulnier firm made beautifully streamlined monoplanes, such as this Type N. To make the wings strong enough they had to be braced by wires to struts above and below. In front of the pilot is a Vickers machine gun, synchronized to fire past the propeller.*

# AIR WAR IN EARNEST

By 1915 large numbers of aircraft on the Western Front carried
machine guns. Most were pushers, but a few had guns
mounted to fire ahead above the propeller.

The Foster mount, for example, put a drum-fed Lewis gun on a curved track above the upper wing of a biplane so that, by releasing the clip, the pilot could pull it down and change to a fresh drum. The trigger was pulled by a Bowden cable, like the brakes on many bicycles.

Unlike other French firms Morane-Saulnier did not build pushers but neat tractor monoplanes. Before the war designer Raymond Saulnier had tried to devise a system to synchronize a forward-firing gun to avoid the propeller, but was defeated by the way the Hotchkiss ammunition often 'hung fire' for a tiny fraction of a second after being fired. His test pilot, Roland Garros, simply fixed narrow steel deflectors to his propeller to deflect the bullets, and between 1-18 April 1915 shot down five enemy aircraft.

Such a thing was unheard-of. When, on 18 April, Garros was shot down by ground fire his secret was out. The famous Dutch aircraft designer Anthony Fokker, employed by Germany, instantly saw that a better answer was a proper synchronization gear. Quickly he perfected one, firing one round from a 500rds/min gun for every four passes of a two-blade propeller turning at 1,000rpm. By June 1915 the Fokker E (*Eindecker* = monoplane) was in service with from one to three synchronized guns.

*Below: Painted black, the four Sopwith Triplanes of B Flight, No 10 (Naval) Squadron, shot down 87 German aircraft between May and July 1917. The pilots were all Canadians.*

*Above: There was nothing magic about triplanes, but the Sopwith example did so brilliantly that many enemy firms copied it. The best was the Fokker Dr.I (dreidecker = three wings). The 'Red Baron' Manfred von Richthofen was killed in one on 21 April 1918, by which time this low-powered (only 110hp) machine was rapidly becoming obsolescent.*

*Below: The Type AI was not one of Morane-Saulnier's best efforts, and wings occasionally parted company despite the profusion of bracing struts. This example, powered by a 120hp Le Rhône rotary engine, was fitted with extra bracing wires as well! Perhaps to show that the wing could stay on, a French pilot looped one 1,111 times in five hours.*

*"British newspapers called the Royal Flying Corps 'Fokker fodder'"*

The result was near-annihilation of Allied aircraft wherever these simple monoplanes went. Previously unknown pilots, such as Oswald Boelcke, Max Immelmann and Ernst Udet became famous aces. The first two studied the distinctly new subject of air combat, and laid down many basic rules. They showed how aircraft could operate in tight groups, dive on the enemy from above (if possible 'out of the Sun', so that they would be hard to see until too late), what manoeuvres to perform and how to break off combat if necessary. Against badly designed Allied aircraft the results were devastating. British newspapers called the Royal Flying Corps 'Fokker fodder'.

# FAMOUS ALLIED FIGHTERS

By 1916 the fighter, often then called a 'fighting scout', was fast becoming the dominant kind of warplane. Most were neat single-seat tractor biplanes, but there were variations.

A few were seaplanes, and many Russian fighters operated on skis in winter. Britain toyed with ungainly anti-Zeppelin fighters intended to loiter waiting for airships, shooting them down with enormous recoilless cannon or various kinds of small bomb (in practice the airships fell to the guns of ordinary fighters, using Pomeroy incendiary ammunition).

The most successful fighter of all was Britain's Sopwith Camel, so called because of its humpbacked appearance with two synchronized Vickers machine guns mounted above a 130hp rotary engine. Though extremely tricky to fly, it was deadly in the hands of an experienced pilot. For 60 years its official score was 1,294; then a British author, Chaz Bowyer, showed that British Camels alone had shot down well over 2,800 enemy aircraft, and hundreds more were added by Camels of Allied forces.

*Below: Partly because of the powerful inbuilt gyroscopic effect of its rotary engine – many types were fitted – the Sopwith Camel was dangerous until a pilot had got used to it. These outstanding fighters were built by 12 British companies, but B3881 was one of a batch of 200 built by Sopwith at Kingston on Thames. Though its pilot is not in Naval uniform, it served with A Flight of No 9 (Naval) Squadron. On the fin is a painting of George Robey, a popular comedian of the day, though this would probably have been lost on the enemy!*

*"The most successful fighter of all was Britain's Sopwith Camel."*

*Right: SPAD produced some of the best fighters of the war. Over 6,000 SPAD VII fighters were followed by 8,440 SPAD XIIIs, and had the war continued a further 10,000 would have been built. This XIII was flown by Capt E.R.Cook of the US Air Service 91st Squadron, who was credited with five victories.*

*Below: D8096 is not a replica but a real, and perfectly restored, Bristol F.2B Fighter ('Fighter' was a registered name). Six of them first went into action on 5 April 1917. They stayed serenely in formation and were hacked to pieces by Richthofen's 'circus'. It was a different story once pilots learned to throw the big Bristol around like a single-seater.*

Another outstanding fighter was the S.E.5a, with a synchronized Vickers plus a Foster-mounted Lewis gun. Its eight-cylinder, water-cooled engine of 200 to 240hp made it one of the fastest fighters of the war at 212km/h (132mph). Similar Hispano-Suiza engines powered the SPAD family, some of which were fitted with a shell-firing cannon firing through the hub of the propeller. Another French family were the Nieuports, among the smallest and most agile machines. They were sesquiplanes (biplanes with one wing much smaller than the other).

A particularly outstanding two-seater was the Bristol Fighter Type F.2B. Thanks to its 250hp Rolls-Royce Falcon engine, it had a performance as good as the single-seaters. Once its pilots had learned to fly it like a single-seater it did well in combat, with the protection of a backseater usually armed with twin Lewis guns. The 'Brisfit' served in the RAF until 1932.

*Though extremely tricky to fly, it was deadly in the hands of an experienced pilot.*

# FAMOUS GERMAN FIGHTERS

In World War I the 'Central Powers' of Germany and
Austro-Hungary tended to build conventional biplane fighters,
armed with two synchronized Spandau machine guns.

The Spandau was derived from the classic Maxim (as was the Allies' belt-fed Vickers). Most 'Hun' fighters were powered by water-cooled, six-cylinder inline engines of 160 or 180hp. Such engines were long and massive, compared with the air-cooled rotaries, and this made fighters less agile in combat. On the other hand they were reliable, and the aircraft were formidable enemies.

Albatros-Werke refined the design of their veneer-skinned fuselages until, with a large propeller spinner

*Below: The Fokker D.VII was in every way quite ordinary; it just added up to Germany's best fighter. Its greatest asset was outstanding manoeuvrability, though it had only two ailerons. This example, with engine covers removed, and an American 'doughboy' in the cockpit, suggests the picture was probably taken after the Armistice.*

added, they were almost perfectly streamlined. This did not make them particularly fast, at 175-188km/h (109-117mph), but they were good all-round machines.

In June 1917 'Red Baron' Manfred von Richthofen, the top scorer of the War, formed some of the first Albatros D.IIIs into the first big 'circus' of four squadrons. Each was painted red, and by 1918 some 'Huns' went in for exotic individual colour schemes. In contrast British RFC and French fighters stayed in sombre camouflage.

LVG were among specialists in two-seaters, while at the end of the war the tiny Siemens-Schuckert D.IV, powered by a 200hp, 11-cylinder, Siemens rotary engine, achieved a rate of climb and ceiling no other in-service aircraft could match. Another outstanding rotary-engined machine that arrived too late was the Fokker D.VIII, very unusual in 1918 in being a parasol (wing above the fuselage) monoplane.

*Below: This LVG C.VI is not a replica but the real thing, and it is still flying after 79 years. The German 'C' category were two-seat fighter/ reconnaissance machines, with long endurance and carrying cameras as well as guns. The C.VI was larger than most, so that even the massive 220hp Benz engine gave only modest performance, but it was an important and successful type.*

*Above: Thanks to a fuselage covered in moulded veneer, the Albatros single-seat fighters looked more like racers. Here a D.Va is seen in company with a Gotha G.V bomber. In April 1918 there were 928 D.Va fighters on the Western Front, 47.6 per cent of the German total. By this time the Albatros was inadequate, and the company was told to make Fokker D.VIIs.*

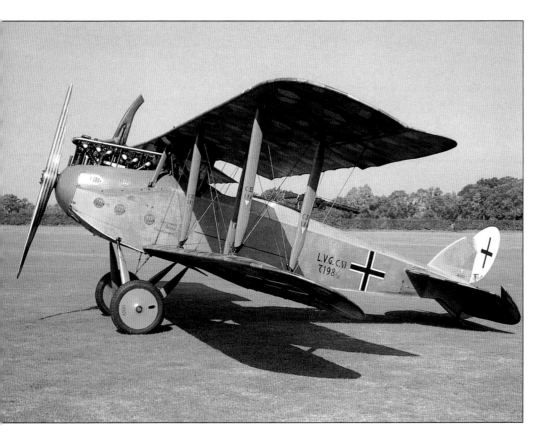

However, in 1918 the top German fighter was the D.VIII's predecessor, the D.VII. By this time Fokker had settled on a fuselage and tail of accurately welded steel tubing, and quite thick wooden wings, everything then being skinned in fabric. Such airframes were easy to make and repair, and very resistant to battle damage.

The D.VII was usually powered by a 160hp Mercedes engine, with a simple car-type radiator on the front. Its all-round qualities were so good that, after the November 1918 Armistice, the Allies especially insisted that every example had to be handed over. Cool Fokker loaded 120 of them, plus about 40 D.VIIIs, into trains and smuggled them to his native Holland where he set up a new factory!

# FIGHTERS OF THE 1920S

Predictably, after what was called 'the war to end wars', the
hectic development of fighters slowed down. Throughout the
1920s most fighters remained simple fabric-skinned biplanes.

Some fighters had all-wood air-frames, many had steel-tube fuselages and a very few were made of aluminium alloy. Whereas during the recent war there had been countless oddballs – for example, with a propeller behind the tail, or a gunner standing terrifyingly in a cockpit in front of a tractor propeller, or with four wings – the post-war fighters were almost all conventional.

Armament tended to remain two synchronized belt-fed machine guns. Mounted above the engine, their breeches were accessible to the pilot so that, if a gun jammed when firing, he could clear the stoppage (a mallet was invariably carried in the cockpit to help). Petrol (gasoline) similar to that used in cars was usually carried in a tank of about 227 litres (50gal, 60 US gal) either in the upper wing or behind the engine. A few fighters had night-flying lighting and even radio.

Apart from the new demand for long trouble-free life, the main advance concerned the engine.

*Above: In the 1920s Emile Dewoitine specialized in all-metal monoplane fighters with a parasol wing (a monoplane wing mounted above the fuselage). He was unable to get orders from his native France, so he built his fighters in Switzerland. Beautifully preserved, this D.27 has a radial engine, but nearly all D.27s had 500hp Hispano-Suiza water-cooled V-12s. During the 1930s Dewoitine at last received French orders, and he produced some of the best fighters in the Armée de l'Air in World War II.*

Rotaries vanished, and in their place came V-12 water-cooled engines or static radials with 9 or 14 cylinders, in each case of at least 400hp. The water-cooled engines looked streamlined, if one ignored the heavy and vulnerable radiator, but the new breed of radials were so much lighter for equal power that in most countries they became almost universal. The most successful were the Bristol Jupiter and Pratt & Whitney Wasp, both with 9 cylinders and rated at about 500hp. From 1925 it became increasingly common for fighter engines to have a supercharger, which at high altitude blew more air into the cylinders and thus increased power.

Most of the impetus for fighter development was provided by racing. As speeds increased, so did the need for aerodynamic cleanliness and a streamlined shape. Extra demands included carriage of light bombs and, for the first naval carrier-based fighters, folding wings, flotation gear and a hook to catch an arrester wire strung across the deck.

*Left: In the 1920s fighters were light enough to be manhandled, especially aboard a carrier. With little fuel on board this Fairey Flycatcher would not have weighed over one ton, so the deck party could grab it and help it slow down on the deck of HMS Furious. Not until 1933 did Royal Navy carriers have transverse arrester wires. The Flycatcher was agile, noisy and loved by its pilots. The engine was a 400hp Armstrong Siddeley Jaguar IV, giving a speed of 216km/h (134mph).*

*Right: In the inter-war years the RAF was called 'the best flying club in the world'. Most pilots knew each other, and were actually paid to cavort in silver biplanes. None better epitomizes this Golden Age of Service-flying than this Bristol Bulldog II, powered by a 440hp Bristol Jupiter. It was delivered in March 1930 and soon wore the black zigzag marking of 17 Sqn.*

# AMERICAN 'PURSUITS'

The United States did not become involved in World War I until 6 April 1917. Its potentially colossal industry was not geared to weapons manufacture.

The US War Department mismanaged aircraft production, to the extent that most of the US Army and Navy squadrons fought with foreign aircraft. Gradually such companies as Curtiss, Thomas Morse, Vought and Douglas grew in strength, not helped by the policy of assigning contracts to whoever was the lowest bidder. Thus, in 1922 Thomas Morse lost out to a tiny firm called Boeing, who won a $1.5 million contract (the largest until 1937) to build 200 Thomas Morse MB-3 scouts.

From then on Boeing never looked back. From 1923 they challenged mighty Curtiss for supremacy across the board. Nearly all the early pursuits –

*Below: The P-12D was a member of a Boeing family which also included the Navy F4B. The 500hp Wasp engine was surrounded by a Townend ring, and fuel capacity could be more than doubled to 462lit (122 US gal) by adding an auxiliary tank under the fuselage, as shown on this aircraft of the 35th Pursuit Squadron. Armament comprised one 'fifty calibre' and two 'thirties', all firing past the cylinders and the Hamilton propeller.*

*Above: The US Army helpfully inscribed the aircraft type and serial number (in this case the 191st aircraft bought with 1928 funds) in these bold letters until 1932, when the information was written in tiny characters on the left side near the cockpit, a practice followed to this day. The P-3A was one of the last aircraft to have an uncowled engine. The 410hp Pratt & Whitney Wasp gave a speed of 246km/h (153mph), but for the 1929 National Air Races aircraft 28-189 was fitted with a long-chord cowling and achieved 299km/h (186mph).*

*Below: This FF-1 was the first aircraft made by the Grumman company. Ordered hesitatingly by the Navy in April 1931, it was flown on 29 December of that year and proved outstanding. Its novel feature was that, laboriously, the landing gear could be cranked up into recesses in the fuselage to reduce drag. Another unusual feature was the transparent enclosure, with sliding hoods, over the pilot and observer. The 575hp Wright Cyclone engine had a ring cowl and drove a Hamilton propeller. Called Fifi by its crews, the FF reached 319km/h (198mph).*

*From 1923 Boeing challenged mighty Curtiss for supremacy across the board.*

the US term for a fighter – were powered by heavy water-cooled engines, the Curtiss V-12 types being dominant. In 1925 a new firm, Pratt & Whitney Aircraft, began testing the Wasp 9-cylinder radial. Rated at 425hp, and later developed to give 600hp, this much lighter engine made possible better fighters, and Vought, Boeing and even Curtiss took full advantage of it. Curtiss also used the bigger Wright Cyclone radial of 750hp in the final versions of its Hawk biplanes.

In 1926 a British aerodynamicist, H.C.H. Townend, perfected a simple form of ring with a curved wing-like profile which, wrapped round a radial engine, dramatically reduced drag. It was first flown in 1928 on a Curtiss trainer, and had the same effect as if the engine's power was increased from 220 to 303hp! Such cowls quickly became standard on US pursuits, and later on many other aircraft. Typical examples were seen on the Boeing F4B of the US Navy and the same company's P-26A of the Army.

The P-26 was one of the first all-aluminium monoplanes, though it had bracing struts and fixed landing gear. A pioneer of retractable landing gear was a newcomer, Grumman, whose FF of 1931 was in consequence able to reach 314km/h (195mph), even though it was a two-seat biplane designed to fly from Navy carriers. In 1934 the single-seat F2F reached 372km/h (231mph). Like most Navy fighters, these portly biplanes carried two 45kg (100lb) bombs as well as two machine guns, one '30 calibre' and the other a much more powerful '50 calibre' (12.7mm, 0.5in) weapon.

# THE LAST BIPLANES

In the 1930s, despite the swift dominance of the monoplane, many designers still believed in the biplane. Such aircraft were generally lighter, more agile and able to use smaller airfields without paved runways.

Most pilots insisted on having an open cockpit so that they could crane their necks to search the sky for enemies, especially any coming up from astern. Not least of the attractions of nimble biplanes was that they were much cheaper than the complicated monoplanes.

Among the greatest builders of such aircraft was Italy's Fiat. The CR.30 and 32 were distinguished by Warren-type (zig-zag) bracing between the wings. They had water-cooled V-12 engines, but the CR.42 of 1938 switched to a 14-cylinder radial of 858hp, giving a speed of 430km/h (267mph). By 1940 it was realized such machines were obsolete, yet the CR.42 fought almost to the end of World War II.

So too did Britain's Gloster Gladiator. This was the eventual winner of a Specification issued in 1930, but the officials spent so long trying to decide what was needed that no Gladiator reached the RAF until 1937. Whereas the CR.42 had two heavy 12.7mm guns, the Gladiator had traditional rifle-calibre (7.7mm,

0.303in) guns, but it did at least have four, the two extra guns being under the lower wings. The Fleet Air Arm used a carrier-based version. The distinguished wartime career of these aircraft really reflected the courage and skill of their pilots.

*Below: With landing gear retracted, this Grumman F3F-2 proclaims its identity as Navy serial 0975, serving as airplane No 6 of Marine Corps fighter squadron VMF-2. The tube in front of the pilot was the optical sight for aiming the two guns, one 'fifty' and one 'thirty'.*

*Right: The Polikarpov I-153 was the ultimate biplane fighter, with outstanding agility, powerful armament and a speed of 427km/h (265mph). A single Moscow factory delivered 3,437 in 1939-41, but even at the start of production such aircraft were obsolescent. Their only advantages were toughness, ability to carry bombs and the newly developed rockets, and reliability in the harshest conditions. This example was captured by Finland, whose insignia was a blue swastika.*

*Below: For sheer piloting enjoyment nothing could surpass the Gloster Gladiator. Its neat landing gear was possible because George Dowty invented an internally sprung wheel, thus starting what has now become a mighty industrial enterprise. Shuttleworth's Gladiator wears the code letters of 247 Sqn.*

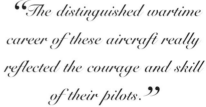

*"The distinguished wartime career of these aircraft really reflected the courage and skill of their pilots."*

In the Soviet Union Nikolai Polikarpov had pioneered the monoplane with the I-16 (p.40), but in the Spanish Civil War these tricky aircraft were out-manoeuvred by CR.32 biplanes. Accordingly Polikarpov persisted with biplanes, culminating in the I-153 which had retractable landing gear, an engine of 1,100hp, four exceptionally fast-firing machine guns and the ability to drop light bombs or fire rockets. Despite this, combats with Japanese monoplanes in 1939 showed that even the I-153 was outdated.

Last of the US Navy biplane fighters, the Grumman F3F entered service from 1936. The final versions had a speed of 423km/h (263mph) on the 850hp of a Wright Cyclone radial, which was good considering all the naval equipment they had to carry. Like their predecessors, the landing gears retracted upwards into the rotund fuselage.

# CURTISS MONOPLANES

The 1930s saw dramatic developments in aircraft design.
Engines grew from 500 to 1,000hp, with 2,000hp in prospect.

Instead of having two blades of carved wood, most propellers had three metal blades whose pitch (angle to the airflow) could be varied from fine for maximum power at take-off to coarse for high-speed flight. Structures became all-metal 'stressed skin', which opened the way to streamlined monoplanes devoid of struts and wires. Such aircraft landed faster than before, so hinged flaps were added under the wings to assist braking, and the cockpit was covered by a transparent canopy.

Landing gears were made retractable, and appeared in various forms.

*Below: Originally the idea of the American Volunteer Group fighting the Japanese in China, shark's teeth have been painted on almost every one of the numerous Curtiss P-40 Kittyhawks still flying. Many also have the Chinese wing markings as used by the AVG, one example being this P-40E, which actually has US civil registration NX40PE and insignia of the 76th FS, 23rd FG.*

*Above: These Curtiss P-36Cs of the 27th Pursuit Squadron were all given different camouflage schemes for the 1939 Air Races, and never appeared thus in any war manoeuvres. Powered by 1,200hp Pratt & Whitney Twin Wasp engines, these tough fighters each had one 'fifty' and three 'thirty'guns, two of the latter being in the wings.*

While Grumman continued to wind them up by screwjack into the fuselage, Seversky pivoted them back into 'bathtub' fairings, while Curtiss retracted the legs backwards while the wheels turned through 90° to lie flat inside the wings just in front of the hydraulically powered flaps. Like the rivals just mentioned, by 1934 Curtiss was ready for streamlined monoplanes of stressed-skin construction. The prototype Model 75 flew on 15 May 1935.

After much development large numbers were built with either a Cyclone or Twin Wasp radial engine of 1,000-1,200hp as the P-36 for the US Army, the Hawk 75 for the French, the Mohawk for the RAF, and in many other export versions. They had from two to six machine guns, and typically reached about 504km/h (313mph).

In October 1938 the tenth P-36 took off as the prototype XP-40 with a 1,090hp Allison V-12 liquid-cooled engine. From this stemmed a profusion of derived aircraft called Tomahawks and Kittyhawks. They were all powered by the Allison or the British Rolls-Royce Merlin, and most had the effective armament of six 12.7mm (0.5in) guns in the wings, outboard of the propeller disc. Almost all could carry a bombload of 227kg (500lb) or 318kg (700lb).

The bombload was useful, because most of the 13,738 aircraft of the P-40 family were used mainly in attack on surface targets. Though nice to fly and exceedingly tough, they were based on a 1934 airframe, and were outclassed by the German and Japanese fighters they were likely to meet.

# HAWKER FIGHTERS

Hawker Aircraft was the 1919 successor to the

Sopwith company.

Its biplane fighters of the 1920s perfected a method of construction based on tubes made from aluminium-alloy strip passed through rollers to form complex channels which were then joined to form the tube. The result was light, strong and easy to repair.

Apart from this, and the 525hp water-cooled Rolls-Royce Kestrel engine, the Fury of 1932 resembled a fighter of 1918. But on 6 November 1935 the prototype Hurricane flew. It was a clean monoplane with a 1,030hp Merlin engine, flaps, enclosed cockpit and inwards-retracting landing gear. In the wings were eight machine guns. Hawker began making 1,000 before any were ordered, and so just enough were available to win the Battle of Britain in 1940. By this time Hurricanes

*Below: Without the Hawker Hurricane the RAF would not have had the slightest chance of winning the Battle of Britain. The last one built, PZ865* Last of the Many *(a play on an epic film,* First of the Few*) is a Mk IIC with four 20mm cannon. Here it is seen with guns removed, six (instead of three) exhaust pipes on each side and an odd mix of red spinner and Middle East camouflage, with red (instead of yellow) tape over where eight Brownings would have been in a Mk I.*

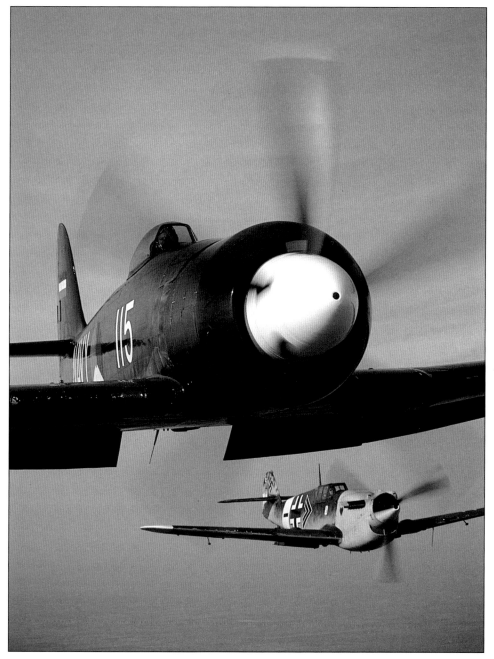

*Above: Despite having a lengthened forward fuselage to house more fuel, the Tempest often carried drop tanks, like this trio from 501 Sqn. The wing was thinner than that of the Typhoon, enabling the Tempest to dive faster without running into shockwave buffeting, and the short-barrel Mk V guns fitted entirely inside the wing. On reflection, the huge projecting barrels of the Typhoon's guns must have frightened the enemy!*

*Right: With flaps lowered to formate on the slow photographic aircraft, this Sea Fury is the property of Concorde captain John Bradshaw. Like some of the most powerful Spitfires, the Centaurus sleeve-valve engine needed a five-bladed propeller to absorb its power. In the background is another regular on the display circuit, a Hispano HA-1112, a Spanish development of the Bf 109 powered by a Merlin engine.*

had modern metal-skinned wings and constant-speed (automatically controlled variable-pitch) propellers. By 1941 Hurricanes had four 20mm cannon and carried bombs. Of 14,231 built, 1,451 were made in Canada.

With the Typhoon the structure was modernized, and the snub nose housed a 2,200hp Napier Sabre 24-cylinder engine. Gloster made nearly all the 3,330 Typhoons, which were disappointing as fighters but devastating as attack aircraft carrying

four 20mm guns, eight rockets or two 454kg (1,000lb) bombs. Later Typhoons introduced a frameless sliding 'bubble' canopy.

Those who flew it would say that at the end of World War II the Tempest was the Allies' best fighter. It was basically a Typhoon with a thinner wing which, to make room for four cannon inside it, had an elliptical shape like a Spitfire. The Tempest II was powered by a Bristol Centaurus 18-cylinder radial of 2,520hp, and the

*"Those who flew it would say that the Tempest was the Allies' best fighter."*

same engine powered the post-war Fury and Sea Fury. These were basically Tempests with a smaller wing and raised cockpit. In Korea these 740km/h (460mph) carrier-based aircraft even shot down several much faster MiG-15s!

# MESSERSCHMITT BF 109

On 6 May 1935 test pilot 'Bubi' Knötsch took off from
Augsburg in the prototype Bf 109. Bayerische Flugzeugwerke
had previously made light civil machines, but this looked
more like a racer, with a stressed-skin structure.

The wing was small, but fitted with slats and slotted flaps, and the landing gears retracted outwards. A *Luftwaffe* general exclaimed 'It will never make a *fighter*!'. Designer Willy Messerschmitt was to prove him very wrong.

Early versions had a 635hp engine and three machine guns, and did well in the Spanish Civil War. When World War II began, the standard version was the Bf 109E, with a 1,175hp DB 601 inverted-V engine cooled by shallow radiators integrated with the

flaps under the wings. Usual armament was two 20mm cannon in the wings and two machine guns above the engine. It was formidable, but a well-flown Spitfire could turn tighter.

The Bf 109F of 1941 had a cleaned-up appearance and slightly more

power. Many ace pilots considered this the best version, even though a year later the 109G introduced the DB 605 enginc of 1,175hp, with 1,800hp briefly available with a 50/50 mix of methanol and water injected into the cylinders. The G could be fitted with a vast assortment of weapons, including two 13mm heavy machine guns above the engine, a 20mm or 30mm cannon firing through the propeller hub and a gondola under each wing housing a further 20mm cannon. Various bombs or rockets could be hung underneath.

Over 14,000 Bf 109Gs were made in 1944 alone, bringing the total of this version to an unknown figure in excess of 30,000. Many other versions were made over a 25-year period in Germany, Hungary, Romania, Czechoslovakia, Switzerland and

Spain. This is despite the fact that most versions suffered from severe shortcomings. Pilots had to get used to these before they could use the Bf 109 as an efficient killing machine.

*Above: A famous photograph of the wing adjutant of JG54 Grünherz (green heart) on his way to deliver an SC250 (551lb) bomb on the Eastern Front in 1942. His aircraft at that time was an Emil Bf 109E-4/B, which by then was becoming obsolescent.*

*Left: Running up the DB 601E engine of a Bf 109G-0. The G-0 retained the smaller engine because the DB 605 was not yet available, but it had the bigger oil cooler underneath. Note the steel tube inserted through the lifting holes at the tail, with a weight attached to keep the tail down.*

*Above: Undoubtedly the most famous Bf 109 in the world is 'Black 6', a Bf 109G-2 Gustav captured in North Africa in 1942 and beautifully restored in its original JG77 livery by Russ Snadden's team at Benson, England. Appropriately, its civil registration is G-USTV.*

# SPITFIRE

In 1936 a prototype aircraft flew for the first time – it was
the legendary Spitfire.

In 1934 Supermarine were testing the Type 224 fighter for the RAF. Then Rolls-Royce announced the Merlin engine of some 1,000hp, while the RAF decided that future fighters should have the unprecedented armament of eight machine guns. Supermarine started afresh on the Type 300. It was to become perhaps the most famous fighter of all time.

Flown on 5 March 1936, the prototype was a sleek, stressed-skin machine, with underwing radiators and outwards-retracting landing gear. Its handling qualities were almost perfect, almost the only problem being

*Below: Messerschmitts would hate to see a Spitfire IX from this angle, and especially this close! The Mk IX was a hasty lash-up, with the two-stage Merlin and two equal-size radiators fitted into a Mk V airframe. The properly engineered aircraft was the beautiful Mk VIII, but sheer pressure on production just kept the factories building the IX, until there were 5,665 of them!*

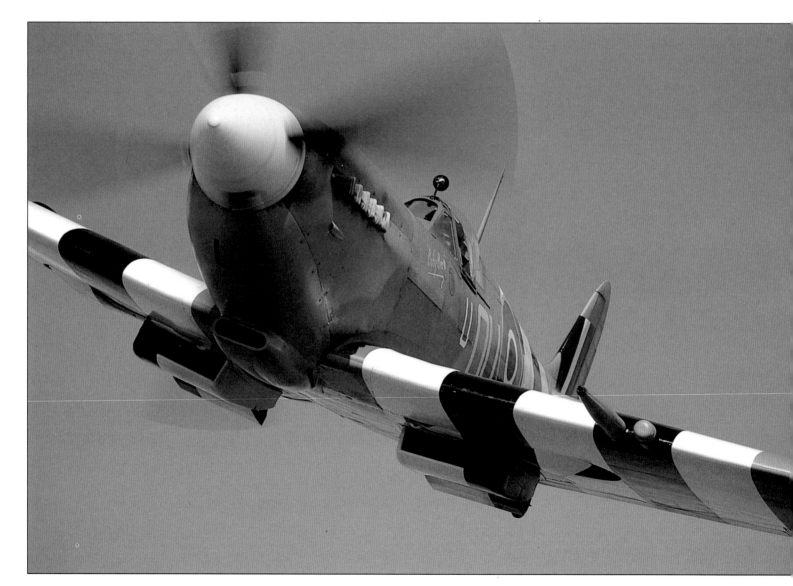

*"Its handling qualities were almost perfect."*

that, as speed increased, rate of roll was reduced until at 644km/h (400mph) the ailerons felt almost immovable. This was a common fault, and the Spitfire's greatest adversary, the Bf 109, was even worse.

In 1940 Spitfires in the Battle of Britain were just getting constant-speed propellers, which Britain had omitted to develop earlier. A handful of Mk IB aircraft had two 20mm cannon and four machine guns, and this became the commonest armament throughout the war. In 1942 Rolls-Royce produced a Merlin engine with a two-stage supercharger. This increased the Spitfire's speed by some 100km/h (62mph) and raised the ceiling by nearly 3,000m (10,000ft)!

The characteristic elliptical wing was based on a strong leading edge and a single spar made of a stack of square tubes one inside the other, tapering to a channel and then to a plain angle towards the tip. Some aircraft had the tips left off for better agility at low level, while high-altitude versions had them extended to pointed tips. After 1943 some versions had the 2,375hp Griffon engine, driving a big five-blade propeller, with metal-skinned ailerons, a larger tail and 'teardrop' canopy.

*"It was to become perhaps the most famous fighter of all time."*

Spitfire production totalled 20,334, plus 2,550 carrier-based Seafires. The final versions were more than twice as heavy and twice as powerful as the prototype, and over 160km/h (100mph) faster.

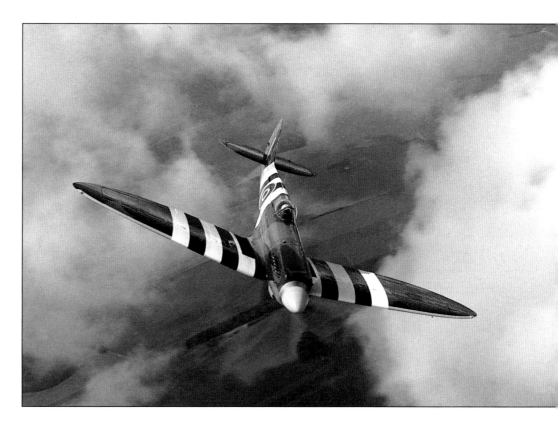

*Above: One of the most beautiful Spitfires was the unarmed Mk XIX, the ultimate photo-reconnaissance version. Powered by the 2,050hp two-stage Griffon, it could carry 1,918lit (422gal) of fuel, compared with 386lit (85gal) for a Spitfire I. The black/white stripes were painted on over 100,000 Allied aircraft on 3-4 June 1944 ready for D-Day, the invasion of Hitler's Europe on 6 June.*

*Below: Marred only by having a very non-standard propeller, and one exhaust pipe per cylinder, instead one for each pair, this Spitfire IA is one of the oldest of the species still flying. Here it wears the code QV for 19 Squadron, which back in July 1938 at Duxford had been the first to receive what was then a new and challenging fighter, very different from their Gloster Gauntlets!*

# THE BATTLE OF FRANCE

Between the World Wars there were well over 100 French
aircraft companies. In 1936 a Socialist government abruptly
nationalized those making military aircraft, which caused
chaos in the production programmes.

On top of this, Communists tried to make sure that each fighter coming off the assembly line lacked a propeller, or some other vital part. Thus, the *Armée de l'Air* was seriously weakened in its desperate fight in spring 1940.

Moreover, its fighters were in most respects inferior to the enemy's Bf 109E. The most numerous was the MS.406C, produced by the Morane-Saulnier firm which had made fighters since 1914. It had a traditional steel tube and fabric fuselage, but wings skinned in plywood bonded to aluminium sheet. Among its deficiencies were a Hispano-Suiza V-12 engine of only 860hp and armament of one 20mm cannon and two machine guns. Top speed was only 465km/h (289mph).

The only other fighters available in numbers – apart from the American

*Below: Against the tide of ever greater engine power, the Caudron company designed the tiny C.714 on the basis of a series of racers, powered by a six-cylinder air-cooled Renault engine of only 450hp. Armament comprised four 7.5mm machine guns in twin packages under the wings. The* Armée de l'Air *initially rejected the C.714, so Caudron began selling them to Finland. Eventually at least 56 did reach the French air force, where in May 1940 they were flown by Polish pilots who had managed to escape to France. Frankly, the C.714 was inadequate.*

Curtiss Hawk 75 – were the Bloch 151 and 152. Almost identical, these had stressed-skin construction, a Gnome-Rhône radial engine of 1,180hp and quite good armament of two 20mm cannon and two machine guns. They were also tough and reasonably manoeuvrable, but suffered from poor all-round performance (speed was 500km/h, 311mph) and each cannon had only 60 rounds of ammunition.

Marginally the best fighter was the Dewoitine D.520. This company had built excellent monoplane fighters from the 1920s, many having a 20mm gun firing through the hub of the propeller. The D.520 had such a gun, as well as four machine guns in the wings. A 947hp Hispano-Suiza engine gave a speed of 535km/h (332mph), and the D.520 was almost the equal of a Bf 109E in manoeuvrability, but only one *Groupe de Chasse* had become operational when the Germans invaded on 10 May 1940.

*Above: The best of the mixed bag of fighters available in May 1940 was the Dewoitine D.520. Considerable numbers survived the German invasion to serve the Vichy collaborative air force, as seen here, as well as the air forces of Germany, Italy and Bulgaria. Sadly, French D.520s fought Allied aircraft, notably over Syria and Algeria, in the same way that French bombers bombed Gibraltar.*

*Below: A second-rate fighter was better than nothing at all, and by the final French collapse in June 1940 Morane-Saulnier had delivered 1,037 M.S.406 fighters. Problems included inadequate engine power (resulting in poor performance) and weak armament. The best of the family were some used by Finland, which fitted them with more powerful Russian M-105 engines.*

# THE RADICAL BELL FIGHTERS

In 1935 Consolidated Aircraft – which had built outstanding
two-seat monoplane fighters – moved from Buffalo,
New York, to California.

Many employees, led by Larry Bell, stayed behind to build fighters of unconventional design.

First, flown in September 1937, came the XFM-1 and YFM-1 Airacudas. Powered by two 1,090hp Allison engines in pusher nacelles, each had a gunner with a 37mm cannon in the front of each nacelle! Various smaller guns were in the fuselage.

Three Airacudas were among the first fighters with tricycle (nosewheel) landing gears. Nosewheel gear was used again in the XP-39 Airacobra, flown in April 1938. This had the Allison engine above the wing, driving

*Below: An unusual view of an Airacobra, which emphasizes the fact that the wing had to be further back than usual because the massive engine was behind the cockpit instead of in the nose. The aircraft shown is the first of 12 YP-39 pre-production fighters, first flown in September 1940. Over 454kg (1,000lb) heavier than the XP-39 prototype, the performance suffered.*

Above: One of the strangest fighters ever built, the Bell Airacuda was planned as a long-range destroyer of bombers. The example shown was the first YFM-1, first flown on 28 September 1939 shortly after World War II began. Soon a turbosupercharger exploded, so later Airacudas had ordinary low-altitude Allison engines, giving a maximum speed of 435km/h (270mph).

Above: This Bell XP-59A Airacomet, US Army Air Force serial 42-108784, was the first jet aircraft built in the United States. Powered by two Whittle-type turbojets made by General Electric, it first flew on 2 October 1942. It is seen here at the new and secret desert test centre called Muroc on the previous day, when it made fast taxi runs and short hops. Later it was fitted with an open passenger cockpit in the nose.

the propeller via a long shaft passing under the cockpit, which had a car-type door on each side. Armament comprised a 37mm or 20mm cannon firing through the propeller hub, two 12.7mm guns above the nose and either two 12.7mm or four 7.6mm guns in the outer wings. Despite its radical features the P-39 proved successful. Of 9,558 built, 4,773 served with the Soviet Union, which rated them highly. Others served in the Mediterranean and Pacific theatres.

The P-63 Kingcobra, first flown in December 1942, was basically a P-39 with a more powerful Allison engine and a new wing with a 'laminar-flow' profile. Speed was increased from 595km/h (370mph) to 660km/h (410mph). Kingcobras could carry three 227kg (500lb) bombs, and again were popular in the USSR, which received 2,421.

In 1941 USAAF General 'Hap' Arnold was told about Frank Whittle's turbojet engine. Quickly he arranged for it to be made in the USA by General Electric, and Bell built the P-59 Airacomet to use it. The XP-59A flew on 1 October 1942, powered by two I-16 engines of 748kg (1,650lb) thrust each. The P-59 family were large and clumsy, reaching only 658km/h (409mph), but they were the first Allied jet fighters to fly.

# NIGHT FIGHTERS WITH RADAR

In World War I night fighters were primitive. Even fitted with a searchlight it was difficult to find enemy bombers, but by the start of World War II in 1939 the first night fighters were on test with a sensor that worked as well by night as by day: airborne radar.

The first such aircraft to enter service were Bristol Blenheims, originally built as three-seat light bombers. Powered by two 840hp Bristol Mercury radials, they were fitted with AI (Airborne Interception) Mk III radar, which was unreliable and difficult to use. Armament comprised four 7.7mm machine guns in a tray under the fuselage, plus a fifth in a retractable dorsal turret. The maximum speed of about 434km/h (270mph) was slower than many *Luftwaffe* bombers.

In 1941 the Boulton Paul Defiant IA entered service, with four 7.7mm machine guns in a power-driven dorsal turret. In daylight this aircraft proved a failure, because with a wing smaller than that of a Hurricane, and the same engine, and a much greater weight, it was unable to manoeuvre as could a single-seater, such as a Bf 109. However, fitted with AI Mk VI radar it shot down several German bombers in 1941.

It was soon recognized that to carry radar as well as heavy armament a night fighter needed to be a powerful twin-engined aircraft. Before World War II

*Right: The only Bristol Blenheim flying today is seen here painted in the overall black of a night fighter. It is painted to represent the personal aircraft of Wing Commander The Hon. Max Aitken, CO of RAF No 68 Squadron, in early 1941. With extreme difficulty and danger these converted light bombers pioneered the art of intercepting hostile aircraft on the darkest night by using the new invention of airborne radar.*

*"The first such aircraft to enter service were Bristol Blenheims."*

Left: Having failed in the Battle of Britain, and with the Me 210 in prospect, the Bf 110 was phased out of production in 1941. Unexpectedly, the Me 210 was a disaster, and the old 110 had to be put back into production. Soon it was found to be an excellent night fighter. This Bf 110G-4c/R3 was the penultimate version, though burdened by a clumsy radar antenna on the nose called Hirschgeweih (stag's antlers).

*"It was soon recognized that to carry radar as well as heavy armament a night fighter needed to be a powerful twin-engined aircraft."*

the *Luftwaffe* thought the Messerschmitt Bf 110 long-range fighter, powered by two 1,050hp DB 601 engines and armed with two 20mm cannon and four machine guns, would sweep the skies clear of enemy aircraft prior to attacks by bombers. In the Battle of Britain the Bf 110 proved 'easy meat' for Hurricanes and Spitfires, but later versions continued in production as night fighters. Powered by 1,475hp DB 605 engines, the Bf 110G night fighters had clumsy antenna arrays on the nose and flame-damped exhausts, but they were still faster than RAF 'heavies'.

Above: Many Boulton Paul Defiants were converted into black-painted night fighters, though initially without the specially developed AI Mk VI radar. Here one is seen with the turret rotated to fire over the pilot's cockpit, whose canopy fairing retracted automatically (normally the canopy and turret were faired together to reduce drag). The Defiant was a nice enough aircraft, but without radar even two pairs of eyes seldom found targets at night. In early 1941 the radar arrived. Provided it worked, the Defiant did well, despite its weak armament, scoring a number of kills. This particular aircraft, Defiant I T4106, was later shipped to the USA.

# LATER NIGHT FIGHTERS

It is difficult to explain why, having for years watched the growing threat of the *Luftwaffe*, the British Air Staff did nothing to equip the RAF with long-range, twin-engined fighters which could, in due course, carry radar.

It was left to the Bristol Aeroplane Co to propose such an aircraft, derived from the Beaufort torpedo bomber. The resulting Beaufighter, first flown in July 1939, was the obvious 'missing aircraft'.

Powered by two 1,635hp Bristol Hercules engines, it had the devastating armament of four 20mm cannon and six machine guns. Night-fighter versions were initially fitted with AI Mk IV radar, with dipole transmitting antennas on the outer wings and a harpoon receiver on the nose, and then with AI Mk VII with a power-driven centimetric-wave dish in a nose radome.

AI Mk IV radar was fitted to the even better de Havilland Mosquito II, which had four cannon and four machine guns all in the nose. With two Merlin engines it reached 595km/h (370mph), much faster than a 'Beau'. Later night-fighter versions of this superb all-wood aircraft reached 682km/h (424mph). Some had the excellent US-developed SCR-720 radar, which was also fitted to the first aircraft designed from the outset to carry radar, the Northrop P-61 Black Widow. This enormous all-black aircraft was powered by two 2,250hp Pratt & Whitney Double Wasp engines,

*"Formating below the defenceless belly of an RAF 'heavy', the pilot could aim a devastating burst at the bomber's wing spars."*

and its central nacelle housed four cannon and sometimes four 12.7mm guns in a dorsal turret.

The best of the *Luftwaffe* night fighters were different versions of the Ju 88G, powered either by BMW 801 radials or Jumo 213 inverted-V engines, in either case in the 2,000hp class. Despite their size, with radar and flame dampers removed many Ju 88Gs could exceed 644km/h (400mph). Most had batteries of forward-firing cannon, plus two more firing up at a steep angle. Formating below the defenceless belly of an RAF 'heavy', the Ju 88G pilot could aim a devastating burst at the bomber's wing spars.

*Left: An official portrait of V8322, one of a batch of 129 Bristol Beaufighter Mk IF night fighters built in 1941. The Hercules engines had sleeve valves and made a soft booming sound (in 1942 the Japanese called the 'Beau' Whispering Death). Night-fighter versions had long flame-damping exhaust pipes, seen here. The pilot sat behind the engines, and some way behind him was the radar operator, who in early examples also reloaded the drum-fed cannon. The circular inlet on the leading edge is an oil cooler.*

Right: The Junkers Ju 88 was the most versatile aircraft in Hitler's Luftwaffe, and a superb machine in almost every way. After 1943 the emphasis was entirely on night-fighter versions, such as this Ju 88G-1, whose clumsy radar antennas were thrust through the night sky by two 1,700hp BMW 801D radial engines.

Below: The superb Mosquito was entirely the result of private enterprise by de Havilland. Here an NF.II night fighter shows off its nose harpoon transmitter, with dipole receivers on the wingtips. Armament was outstanding, four cannon and four machine guns all in the nose.

# US NAVY FIGHTERS

At the start of World War II in 1939, the most important
US Navy fighter was the Grumman F4F Wildcat.

Started as another biplane, with landing gear cranked up into the tubby fuselage, it was fortunately modified into an agile monoplane with a big folding wing. Though it had only 1,200hp, its manoeuvrability and (in most versions) six heavy 12.7mm guns made it formidable. Production totalled 7,815, of which 920 were used by Britain's Fleet Air Arm.

The rival Brewster F2A Buffalo was inferior, whereas Grumman went on with the F6F Hellcat, which can fairly be called 'the fighter that defeated the Japanese'. Powered by a 2,000hp Pratt & Whitney Double Wasp, this tough and agile fighter usually had the same armament as the Wildcat but at 605km/h (376mph) was much faster, and it could also carry radar for night fighting.

A close counterpart was the perhaps even better Vought F4U Corsair, notable for its bent 'inverted-

*"The F6F Hellcat can fairly be called 'the fighter that defeated the Japanese'."*

Below: Quite a few of the 12,571 F4U Corsairs are still flying today. One of the most familiar in the UK is this example of the final production type, the F4U-7, 94 of which were supplied to the French Aéronavale. Armament included four 20mm cannon and up to 1,814kg (4,000lb) of bombs. The black/yellow stripes denote service at Suez in 1956.

gull' wing. Fitted like the F6F with a Double Wasp engine and landing gears which retracted backwards into the wing, the F4U had six 12.7mm or four 20mm guns and also carried bombs or rockets, yet some versions reached 756km/h (470mph). Production continued until 1952, totalling 12,571.

Grumman's F7F Tigercat had over 4,000hp from two Double Wasps, and it proved too much for operation from carriers. Only modest numbers were made of various night-fighter and reconnaissance versions, typically reaching 700km /h (435mph) even with four 20mm and four 12.7mm guns plus radar. In contrast, Grumman's final piston-engined fighter, the F8F Bearcat, was a small machine with just four guns (12.7mm or 20mm), designed for the utmost agility. Engine was again a Double Wasp.

Just too late for the war, Ryan delivered a batch of FR-1 Fireballs. They were fitted with a 1,350hp Cyclone piston engine, plus (for use in combat) a 726kg (1,600lb) thrust turbojet.

*Above: In the F6F Hellcat's first big engagement, on 4 December 1943, 91 of them met 50 Japanese A6M 'Zeros' and destroyed 28, for the loss of two. By VJ-Day, the end of World War II, US Navy carrier-based aircraft had destroyed 6,477 Japanese aircraft. Of this total, 5,155 were victims of this pugnacious Grumman product – and all in the final 21 months.*

*Below: One Double Wasp engine would have seemed most impressive early in World War II, so one can imagine the thoughts of Navy and Marines aviators when they found the F7F had two! This F7F-3, formerly US Navy BuNo 80483, is well known on the European circuit, painted in original Midnight Blue. Some Tigercats were two-seat night fighters fitted with radar in an extended nose.*

# THE GREAT PATRIOTIC WAR

This is what the Soviet Union called World War II, which for
them began when Germany invaded on 22 June 1941.

Hitler believed he could defeat the USSR quickly, and for a while it looked as if he would. Many thousands of Soviet aircraft were soon destroyed, mainly on the ground, and the *Luftwaffe* had almost complete command of the air.

In 1934 the Polikarpov I-16 had been the first fighter with a cantilever monoplane wing and retractable landing gear, but this stumpy machine had traditional structure and was not only tricky to fly but by 1941 was outclassed. Mikoyan and Gurevich achieved only limited success with the MiG-3, and Lavochkin and two colleagues had such trouble with the LaGG-3 – like other Soviet fighters, made mainly of wood – that LaGG was said by its pilots to mean '*Lakirovannii Garantirovannii Grob*', varnished guaranteed coffin!

By 1942 Lavochkin had re-engined the LaGG with the excellent 1,700hp ASh-82 radial, and the resulting La-5 at last began to beat the 109s and 190s. Armament was typically two 20mm cannon above the fuselage, and speed 648km/h (403mph). The 9,920 La-5s were followed by the part-metal La-7

*"All were tough, easily repairable and able to dogfight with anything in the Luftwaffe."*

*Below: This Polikarpov I-16 is probably a Type 18 version, made in 1938-39. Unlike close relatives it had just four fast-firing ShKAS machine guns, other versions having two 20mm cannon in the wings. Even by this time this basically 1933 design was completely outclassed by later fighters, yet large numbers were still being built when Hitler's Panzer divisions invaded in 1941. Total production was 9,450. As might be expected from its appearance, the I-16 was also a very tricky aircraft to fly.*

and the La-9 with the devastating armament of four powerful 23mm guns, all in the fuselage.

Greatest of the wartime fighter designers was A.S. Yakovlev. The Yak-1 of 1939 was powered by an M-105 V-12 engine of 1,100hp, and similar engines of 1,210-1,260hp powered the Yak-7, Yak-9 and finally the super-agile Yak-3. Most had a cannon of from 20mm up to an awesome 45mm calibre firing through the propeller hub, usually plus a 12.7mm gun above the fuselage. All were tough, easily repairable and able to dogfight with anything in the *Luftwaffe*.

In 1945 the French Normandie-Niemen pilots, who had fought on the Soviet front, chose the Yak-3 in preference to all other Allied fighters to take back to France. Excluding prototypes, total production of these four Yak types was 36,750!

*Above: Yak-9D fighters of a GvIAP (Guards Independent Fighter Regiment) in 1943. The Yak-9D was a long-range version, with extra fuel and oil, armament being a single 20mm ShVAK and one 12.7mm Beresin UBS. Maximum speed at medium altitudes was 591km/h (367mph).*

*Below: These MiG-3 fighters were photographed in the winter of 1941-42 serving with the 12th IAP (fighter aviation regiment) in the defence of Moscow. Some are all-red but most are in winter white, with red wings so that they could be spotted easily after a forced landing.*

# FOCKE-WULF FW 190

Even though the prototype was being tested at Bremen airport
more than three months before World War II, the Fw 190
remained totally unknown to British intelligence until it
was encountered by the RAF in 1941!

To say it was an unpleasant shock is an understatement. Compared with the RAF's main fighter of 1941, the Spitfire VB, the 190 was roughly 56km/h (35mph) faster at all altitudes, it had a much faster rate of roll, and it had the devastating armament of four 20mm cannon and two machine guns.

It was an even greater surprise to find such a formidable fighter powered by an air-cooled radial engine (the 1,600hp BMW 801). When in May 1942 an Fw 190 landed by mistake in Wales the RAF was intrigued by its advanced engineering, its canopy 'giving an unrivalled view', and its totally electric accessory systems which included computer control of the power plant.

Later versions were fitted with over 80 different kinds of armament, including bombs of up to 1,800kg (3,968lb). Some had extra armour for shooting down bombers of the US 8th Air Force, while others were used as night fighters (without radar). By late 1943 the Fw 190D was in service with the 2,060hp Jumo 213F inverted-V liquid-cooled engine, with an extra section added in the rear fuselage to balance the longer nose which ended in a circular radiator. The D-9 was the last main production version, with a

*"It was an even greater surprise to find such a formidable fighter powered by an air-cooled radial engine."*

speed of 686km/h (426mph) and a modified bubble canopy.

Too late for the war, the Fw 190 was developed into a family of fighters called Ta 152. These superficially resembled the Fw 190D, but were redesigned, with hydraulics replacing electrics, and some had the 2,300hp DB 603 engine. Last of all came the Ta 152H high-altitude fighter, with greatly extended span, able to reach 760km/h (472mph) at 12,500m (41,000ft). No aircraft of any of these families is flying today, but an American museum has restored a fine-looking Fw 190D-12.

*Left: This Fw 190A-series is unusual in having had its armament removed. Moreover, though it has a theatre band round the tail, it has no Luftwaffe codes and thus has not been delivered. It is surely extraordinary that, though some 19,400 were constructed, not one Fw 190 remains in flying condition, and almost the only example left in its original condition should be a 'one-off' two-seat conversion! It is also remarkable that most of these superb fighters were used mainly on ground-attack missions, while the ace pilots of the Luftwaffe generally flew the Bf 109, which was inferior on almost every count, except for being cheaper to buy.*

*Left: The best of all 190s were the 'long-nosed' D-series, called Dora by their pilots. The only known survivor is this Fw 190D-12 at the Champlin Fighter Museum in the USA. Powered by a 2,240hp Jumo 213F engine, with a circular nose radiator, it was sent back to Germany to be completely refurbished, though it is unlikely ever to fly again.*

*Below: The first version to go into mass production was the Fw 190A-3, of the type seen here. These examples were serving in early 1942 with 7/JG2 'Richthofen' at Morlaix, France. JG2 served on the Western Front to the end of the war, which denied it the chance of racking up the huge scores often amassed by fighter wings on the Eastern Front. The aircraft flown by III/JG2's adjutant landed in England by mistake.*

# GREAT USAAF FIGHTERS

The P-38 Lightning and P-47 Thunderbolt were great in all senses of the word, including size and weight. The former, flown in January 1939, was unlike anything seen before.

Lockheed studied every possible arrangement of two Allison V-12 engines before deciding on a short central nacelle and twin tail booms behind the engines. Production P-38s had engines of 1,150 and later 1,325hp, with the propellers turning in opposite directions to improve handling. The exhaust was piped to a turbo-supercharger in the top of the boom,

*Below: Seen pristine and polished on factory test before delivery, these Republic Thunderbolts are of the final P-47N variety. They had 2,800hp Double Wasps, a bigger wing, new radio (see antennas), extra fuel and many other new features.*

which made the aircraft uncannily quiet, while the glycol-type coolant was piped to and from radiators on the sides of the booms behind the wing.

Armament was usually one 20mm cannon and four 12.7mm heavy machine guns, and later versions could carry rockets or two 454kg (1,000lb bombs). Most Lightnings escorted bombers, their already long range being stretched by drop tanks containing extra fuel under the inner wings. The P-38 was luxurious, and enjoyable to fly. With strong hands on the 'spectacle' control wheel the rate of roll was far higher than the span of

15.85m (52ft) might have suggested. P-38 production totalled 9,923.

In contrast, the P-47 was preceded by a long series of 'pursuits' produced by Seversky, which in 1939 changed its name to Republic Aviation. All had radial engines, all-metal stressed-skin structure and elliptical wings. The P-47 incorporated the results of studying the first 18 months of World War II. When the prototype flew in May 1941 it was bigger and heavier than earlier single-engined fighters. The 2,000hp Double Wasp engine, driving an enormous four-blade propeller, was supercharged by a giant turbo under the rear fuselage

to which the exhaust was ducted. Armament was no fewer than eight 12.7mm (0.5in) guns in the outer wings. Later versions introduced a 'teardrop' canopy, heavy bomb or rocket loads and engines up to 2,800hp, giving a speed up to 756km/h (470mph). Production was a massive 15,683.

*Below: This Lockheed P-38J, 42-67543, tragically crashed at an airshow in 1996. Features include the turbo housings in the top of each tail boom, the radiators on the sides of the tail booms and the intakes immediately behind the propellers for the oil coolers. To get aboard the pilot simply released the catch on a ladder at the back of the nacelle.*

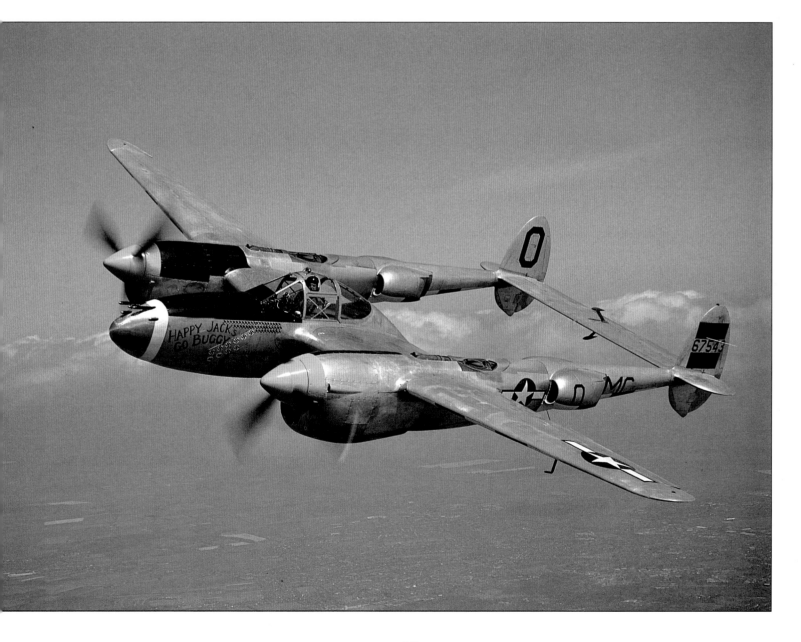

# FLEET AIR ARM FIGHTERS

After the Flycatcher (p.16) came a succession of biplane
fighters differing from their land-based counterparts in having
specific adaptations for their naval role.

These included corrosion-resistant structure, folding wings for stowing in cramped hangars, towing attachments for catapult take-offs, a hook to catch a deck arrester wire on landing, and some form of flotation bag(s) for emergency alighting on the sea.

All this made naval fighters slightly inferior performers. In addition, the problem of finding their tiny floating airfield after a long sortie was considered to demand the carriage of a navigator, which made the fighter's chance of winning a dogfight even worse.

Thus the Fairey Fulmar, first flown in January 1940, was rather like a Hurricane with a second seat. Despite a maximum speed of only 396km/h (246mph), it flew many vital missions from 13 Royal Navy carriers.

In 1941 Fairey flew the first Firefly. This was more formidable, with a Griffon engine of 1,730hp, increased later to 2,250hp, and four 20mm cannon, eight rockets or two 454kg (1,000lb) bombs. Early versions included radar-equipped night fighters, but later marks were primarily anti-submarine aircraft.

Following the carrier-equipped Sea Hurricane came progressively better types of Supermarine Seafire. These were the most important British naval fighters of World War II, and they culminated in 1947 in the Mk 47, with power-folding wings, a 2,375hp

Griffon driving a six-blade contra-rotating propeller, four 20mm guns and either rockets or three 227kg (500lb) bombs. This was the ultimate development of the Spitfire, reaching 727km/h (452mph).

The Blackburn Firebrand (2,500hp Bristol Centaurus) and Westland Wyvern (4,110hp AS Python turboprop) were really torpedo carriers, but the slim de Havilland Hornet (two 2,030hp Merlin) was a long-range

*Above: First flown painted silver, V V430 was the first production Sea Hornet NF.21, with a back-seater to manage the radar. Sea Hornets later received the grey/duck egg colour scheme seen on the Firefly opposite. VV430 survived at Hurn with 771 Sqn until 1955.*

fighter which in Mk 21 form had radar and a navigator. Carrying four 20mm cannon, but without the rockets or bombs, Hornets could reach up to 756km/h (470mph). Tragically, no Hornet of any kind has been preserved.

*Left: There was no other aircraft in service like the Wyvern; it resembled a single-engined 'Bear'! Though it had the shape of a traditional fighter, it stood over 4.6m (15ft) high and weighed over 12 tons, and it could carry four 20mm cannon, a full-size torpedo or a heavy load of bombs or rockets. This Wyvern S.4 is about to thump on the deck of HMS Eagle, in the mid 1950s, with 831 Sqn.*

*Below: Having started with indifferent aircraft penalized by the need for a backseater, the Firefly programme resulted in 1,701 machines of many varieties for a wide range of tasks. This example, preserved in flying condition, was built as an anti-submarine Mk 5, served with the Royal Australian Navy and was then converted as a dual trainer.*

# JAPANESE FIGHTERS

When the Imperial Naval Air Force struck the US Pacific Fleet
at Pearl Harbor on 7 December 1941, ignorance of Japan's
warplanes was almost total.

It was believed that they were all inferior copies of Western types, so encounters with the real aircraft caused shock bordering on panic.

The most numerous fighter (about 10,500 built) was the Mitsubishi A6M, popularly called the Zero. Though it had only 950 to 1,130hp, it was so light that its manoeuvrability was far superior to that of the indifferent Allied fighters ranged against it, and with two 20mm cannon and two machine guns it was very formidable. Not least, with a drop tank it had a range close to 3,220km (2,000 miles), so in three months it helped Japan conquer more territory than any nation had previously in history.

Its counterpart in the Imperial Army was the Nakajima Ki-43.

Though this did not need naval equipment it was inferior in almost all respects, being slower and having only two 12.7mm guns above the nose. Accordingly, Nakajima abandoned 'agility at any price' and in the Ki-44 went for speed (605km/h, 376mph) and firepower (for example, two 20mm or even 40mm cannon and two 12.7mm). Mitsubishi likewise went for

*Below: Japanese aircraft in World War II tended to be conventional in form, but some were outstandingly good. It is generally felt that, possibly excepting the Ki-100, the best Army fighter was the Nakajima Ki-84 Hayate (hurricane). Almost all the Japanese types were delightful to fly, but the Ki-84 also had an outstanding performance and formidable armament, such as two 20mm and two 30mm cannon and two 250kg (551lb) bombs.*

> *"It was believed that they were all inferior copies of Western types, so encounters with the real aircraft caused shock bordering on panic."*

*"Unexpectedly, the resulting Ki-100 was the best Japanese fighter of the entire conflict!"*

*Below: The Air Museum at Chino, California, says that this Mitsubishi A6M5 'Zero' is the only completely authentic flyable example in the world of the fighter that proved such a shock to the Allies in December 1941. Its secret was in being lighter than the opposition. Even this late model weighed only about 2,722kg (6,000lb) loaded, half that of typical British or US fighters, so its 1,130hp engine was by no means inadequate. Designer Jiro Horikoshi became more famous in the USA than any designer of American fighters!*

*Above: The Kawasaki Ki-61 Hien (swallow) was unusual in having a liquid-cooled engine (a copy of the German DB 601A). This engine gave prolonged trouble, but this Army fighter was one of the few Japanese fighters with good performance and a strong airframe. Most had two guns in the fuselage and two in the wings of various calibres, but this Ki-61-I's wing guns cannot be seen.*

speed and firepower with the Navy's racer-like J2M.

Two particularly good fighters were the Navy Kawanishi N1K1-J and N1K2-J and the Army Nakajima Ki-84, both powered by the 18-cylinder Nakajima Homare of 1,990hp. In contrast, Kawasaki used a liquid-cooled engine in the Army Ki-61, but near the end of the war shortage of engines forced a 1,500hp radial to be hurriedly substituted. Unexpectedly, the resulting Ki-100 was the best Japanese fighter of the entire conflict!

Unlike other countries Japan also operated fighter seaplanes. Some were a version of the A6M made by Nakajima, while the best was the N1K1, from which the N1K1-J was developed. Both had a single central float and small floats near the wingtips.

# MUSTANG

In 1940 the British Purchasing Commission signed a contract
with North American Aviation for a fighter of completely new
design. The prototype flew on 26 October of that year.

Production Mustang Is arrived in Britain just over a year later. The RAF was impressed. Compared with a Spitfire V the US import had heavier armament of four 12.7mm (0.5in) and four 7.7mm guns and double the fuel capacity, yet thanks to a 'laminar' wing profile it was on average 56km/h (35mph) faster! The only shortcoming was that the 1,150hp Allison V-12 engine, cooled by a radiator under the rear fuselage, fell off sharply in power at heights over 6,000m (20,000ft).

Accordingly the RAF used Mustang Is as low-altitude reconnaissance fighters, while the first batch for the US Army were P-51s with four 20mm cannon, followed by A-36 attack aircraft with six 0.5in guns, two 227kg (500lb) bombs and dive brakes. Next came P-51As with four 0.5in guns, bombs and drop tanks for long-range escort.

By 1942 it was clear the basic design was brilliant, and an obvious way to overcome the fall in performance at high altitude would be to fit the highly supercharged Merlin engine, made under licence by Packard as the V-1650. The resulting P-51B differed externally in having an intercooler intake under

Above: Looking totally different from the Mustangs that fought in 1941-44, all the publicity today is gained by the swarms of P-51D Mustangs which only got into action in numbers in the final year of the war. This one bears the markings of the crack 336th FS, 4th Fighter Group.

Left: With the P-82 Twin Mustang North American Aviation returned to the Allison V-1710 engine. This example is the second of the P-82E (later F-82E) long-range escort version. The fuselages were longer than those of the P-51.

the nose and a propeller with four broad blades. Though armed with only four 0.5in guns, its 700km/h (440mph) speed and very long range made it the best escort fighter available.

Huge orders were placed, but most were switched to the P-51D with six guns in a better installation, and a clear-view teardrop canopy. With drop tanks and an extra tank behind the cockpit these aircraft could fly to distant Berlin and then defeat the best of the *Luftwaffe!* These later Mustangs were credited with the destruction of over 9,000 *Luftwaffe* aircraft, 4,950 of them in air combat. After building 15,367 Mustangs NAA produced the P-82 Twin Mustang, with twin fuselages, which fought in Korea as a long-range night fighter.

*Below: Bearing the insignia of an aircraft of the famed 354th Fighter Group, this P-51D forms an interesting comparison with the Spitfire LF.XVIe formating with it. Designed more than four years later, the Mustang took advantage of new aerodynamics in the wing and cooling radiator in order to carry up to three times as much fuel yet fly faster on an identical engine. Armament of six 0.5in guns compared with the Spit's two 20mm cannon and two 0.5in or four 0.303in.*

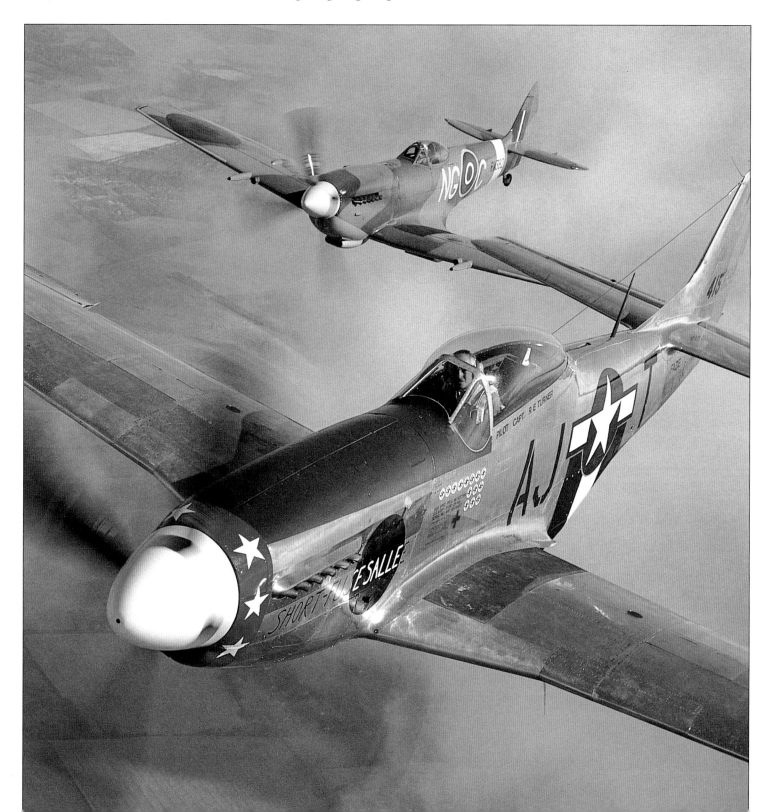

# GERMAN JETS

Englishman Frank Whittle patented the turbojet in 1930, but nobody in his country was interested.

The turbojet, unlike the piston engine and propeller – comprising a compressor, combustion chamber, a turbine driving the compressor and a propelling nozzle – imposes no restriction on aircraft speed.

Whittle was unable to build the first of the revolutionary new engines until 1937. By this time thousands of workers in German aircraft and engine firms were developing jets, and a wide range of different types emerged during World War II.

By far the most important was the Me 262, powered by two Jumo 004B engines of 900kg (1,984lb) thrust each.

With superb handling qualities, a speed of 870km/h (540mph), internal fuel capacity of 2,570 litres (565gal, 679 US gal) and the devastating armament of four 30mm cannon, this aircraft was in many ways the most formidable of the war. It was flawed by dangerous engine unreliability, poor turn radius and very long take-off and landing. Some of the 1,380 built were used as bombers, and a few were two-seat radar-equipped night fighters.

The Messerschmitt Me 163B was a unique tailless fighter powered by a rocket engine, which took off from a jettisonable trolley, climbed steeply to

*"It was flawed by dangerous engine unreliability, poor turn radius and very long take-off and landing."*

*Below: If there had been anyone in a position of authority in Britain in 1929 able to understand the importance of Frank Whittle's jet engine the RAF would have had jet fighters by 1937 at the latest. As it was, when this Me 262A-1a got into action in 1944 the RAF had nothing in the same class. Today a batch of Me 262 replicas are being built in the USA, powered by General Electric J85 engines.*

*"Fantastic performance was achieved at the cost of very short endurance."*

intercept bombers, made a firing pass with two 30mm guns and then glided back to land on a sprung skid. Fantastic performance was achieved at the cost of very short endurance and the use of large tanks of highly corrosive liquids which exploded if they came into contact.

Another last-ditch fighter which made frightening demands on its pilots was the Heinkel He 162. Powered by an 800kg (1,764lb) thrust BMW 003 mounted above the fuselage, this tiny machine was designed, built and tested in the last ten weeks of 1944! With a speed of 905km/h (562mph) and two cannon, the He 162A-2 was planned to be built at the rate of 4,000 per month, but Germany was defeated long before such a production rate was even approached.

*Above: The unique Me 163B Komet rocket-propelled interceptor was far more likely to kill its own pilot than the enemy, mainly because of difficulty of landing on a small retractable skid. Armament was two 30mm cannon in the wing roots. On the nose was a small propeller to drive the electric generator. Factories dispersed against bombing built about 370.*

*Below: An even more frantic last-ditch programme saw the Heinkel He 162 Salamander – also called the Volksjäger, people's fighter – designed, built, flown and put into mass production in ten weeks. Armament was again two 30mm guns, and a high proportion of the airframe was wood. Though a brilliant concept, it was unpleasant to fly, and there was no time to get it right.*

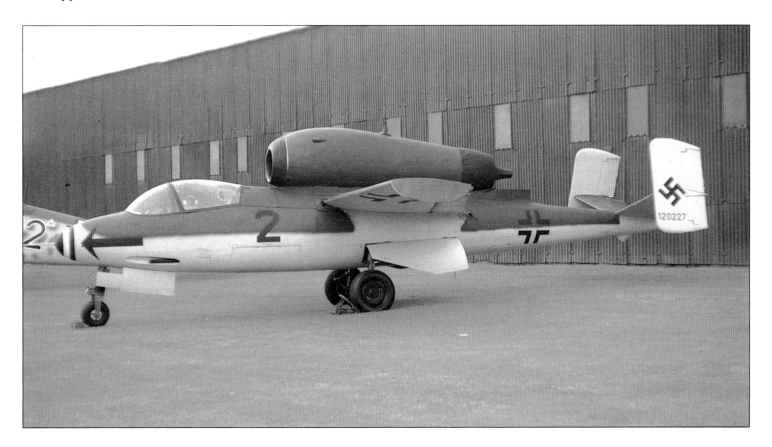

# ALLIED JETS

British bungling of Whittle's brilliant invention was almost total. Having left the harassed RAF officer to find all the money to make his engine himself, the government then handed it over to the Rover Car Co.

This caused such problems that by 1942 development was almost at a standstill. The first four prototypes of the Gloster Meteor twin-jet lacked engines, and it was not until 5 March 1943 that the fifth aircraft was able to fly, powered not by Rover but by de Havilland engines!

Fortunately, in November 1942 Rover were replaced by Rolls-Royce. Overnight, Britain's jets surged ahead, to such purpose that in July 1944 the Meteor I became the first jet fighter in squadron service in the world. Unfortunately it was a rather pedestrian aircraft, reaching only 668km/h (415mph) with two 771kg (1,700lb) thrust Welland engines. Armament comprised four 20mm cannon in the sides of the nose. The Meteor III reached 793km/h (493mph), and at the end of the war the Meteor IV was fitted with Derwent engines uprated to 1,361kg (3,000lb), reaching 933km/h (580mph).

De Havilland's Goblin engine, initially rated at 1,225kg (2,700lb), powered the prototype Vampire on 20 September 1943. This neat and agile machine had an ideal turbojet installation with a short jetpipe made possible by carrying the tail on twin booms. It reached 869km/h (540mph).

De Havilland generously handed the engine for the second Vampire to Lockheed so that the XP-80 Shooting Star could fly on 9 January 1944.

Production P-80s had the 1,814kg (4,000lb) General Electric I-40, and six 12.7mm (0.5in) guns in the nose. They entered service in February 1945, and later versions flew many missions in Korea.

Just too late for the war, the Republic XP-84 Thunderjet flew in February 1946 on the 1,701kg (3,750lb) thrust of a General Electric J35. The air inlet was in the nose, which also housed four 12.7mm guns, two more being in the wings. Republic built 4,457 'plank wing' F-84s, plus 2,713 F-84F fighters with swept wings.

*"In July 1944 the Meteor I became the first jet fighter in squadron service in the world."*

*Below: The Gloster Meteor III differed from the Mk I mainly in having a sliding canopy, instead of a clumsy upward-hinged pattern. These examples, serving with RAF No 56 Squadron immediately after the war, are equipped with flush-fitting belly tanks. The Meteor was a pedestrian design which, by dint of sheer engine power, was kept in production in many versions for ten years.*

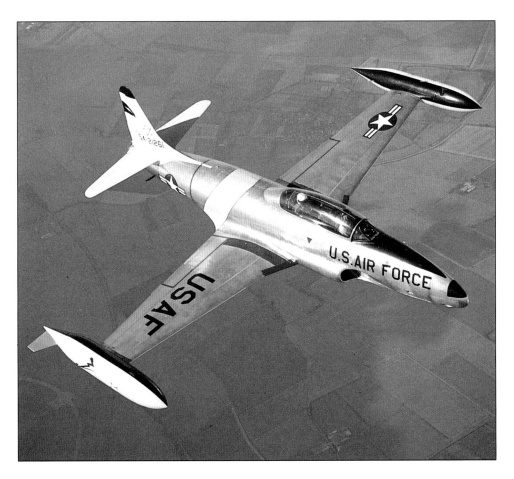

Left: Though the Bell Airacomet was the first American jet, it was far outperformed by the Lockheed P-80 Shooting Star. Large numbers of these, redesignated F 80, were used in the Korean war in 1950-53, by which time these fine aircraft had been developed into the F-94 night fighter and the T-33 trainer. Many Lockheed engineers said to Mac Short, who suggested the trainer version, 'The P-80's a fine airplane, why make it a dodo?' To their astonishment the trainer turned out to be faster than the fighter! This photograph shows one of the preserved T-33 trainer versions.

Below: Having carried out the original design, Gloster handed further development and all production of the Meteor two-seat night fighter to sister-firm Armstrong Whitworth. They had radar in the nose, so the guns were displaced to the wings. Here a Meteor NF.11 is accompanied by a trainer version of the de Havilland Vampire, an agile and cost/effective aircraft of which over 4,200 were built. Like the Meteor, single-seat Vampires were armed with four 20mm cannon.

# COMBAT OVER KOREA

Though the Me 163B and Me 262 appeared to have slightly
swept-back wings, this was for reasons of stability
and control.

Too late for World War II, German aerodynamicists confirmed by testing models in wind tunnels that sweeping the wings back could enable aircraft to fly closer to the speed of sound (called Mach 1), and with the advent of jet propulsion this became very important.

In 1945 North American Aviation received USAAF permission to delay their XP-86 Sabre by a year in order to sweep back the wings and tail at 35°. When the prototype flew on 1 October 1947 it was the most advanced fighter in the world, with hydraulically boosted flight controls, full-span slats,

six 12.7mm (0.5in) guns in the nose, integral tanks formed by sandwich-type wing skins, twin speed brakes on the rear fuselage, and a speed of 1,086km/h (675mph) on the 2,200kg (4,850lb) thrust of a General Electric J47 engine. The first F-86A was delivered to the newly formed USAF in December 1948.

Had this classic aircraft not been produced with such speed the Korean war, which broke out in June 1950, would have seen mastery of the air gained by an unknown Soviet fighter. Stupidly, the British government sent to Moscow the world's most powerful engine, the 2,270kg (5,000lb) thrust Rolls-Royce Nene. In a matter of weeks it was being put into production as the RD-45, while design raced ahead on a swept-back fighter to be powered by it. The resulting Mikoyan-Gurevich MiG-15 was flown on 30 December 1947. It had a mid-mounted wing, high tailplane and armament of one giant 37mm and two 23mm cannon. Performance was similar to that of the F-86, but the Chinese MiG-15 pilots were so inexperienced the combat results were one-sided.

*Left: One of the world's classic fighter designs, an F-86 is seen here firing sixteen 5in HVARs (high-velocity aircraft rockets) at a ground target. Swept-back wings and tail gave the Sabre increased performance, but its designers also made it a beautiful aircraft to fly. It alone could match the MiG-15 in Korea.*

*Right: The Meteor NF.11 night fighter in the rear is a derivative of a fighter designed in 1941, and so could fairly be called a traditional piston-engined aircraft powered by jet engines. In contrast, the F-86A Sabre (British-registered 48-0178 is shown) was designed six years later, and they were six years of amazing development when fighter technology was completely transformed. The Meteor has considerably more engine thrust, but is 160km/h (100mph) slower.*

In the 1950s Britain's best fighter was the tough and graceful Hawker Hunter, which like the Sabre was supersonic in a dive. Usually armed with four 30mm guns, it did not enter service until seven years after the Sabre, and even then was in need of many modifications. Despite this, 1,972 were built for many air forces.

*Below: Made possible by a British engine, which was made little use of in Britain, the MiG-15 was designed and built in a matter of weeks, and made the name 'MiG' front-page news around the world. Including examples built under licence, production exceeded 16,000. This one is a Polish UTI MiG-15 trainer.*

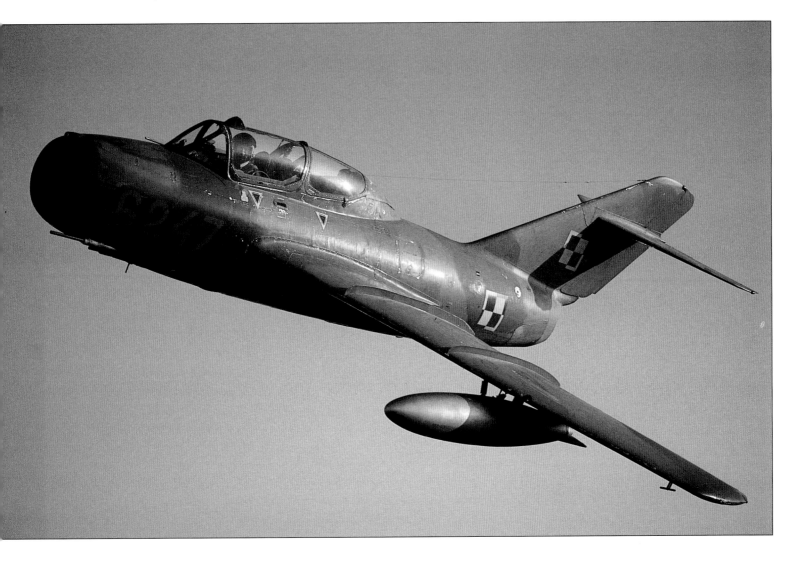

# JET NIGHT FIGHTERS

The first jet night fighters were radar-equipped two-seat
versions of day fighters, such as the Me 262, Meteor, Vampire,
Venom and the Lockheed F-94 derived from the P-80.

All were armed with guns except for the F-94C, which was fitted with a link between the radar and the flight controls to steer the aircraft automatically to intercept from the side. At the appropriate distance a battery of unguided rockets would be fired 'covering an area of sky as large as a football field'.

Purpose-designed night fighters tended to be larger. The USAF used the Northrop F-89 Scorpion, at first armed with six 20mm cannon, then with 104 rockets and finally with guided

*Below: One of the biggest fighters, the Northrop F-89 Scorpion was powered by two Allison J35 engines mounted close together under the fuselage. This is an early F-89A with non-afterburning engines of 2,313kg (5,100lb) thrust and six 20mm guns (and in this photograph ground-attack rockets under the wings).*

missiles. The Navy used the Douglas F3D Skyknight, with pilot and radar operator side-by-side; this had four 20mm cannon, and after 1955 some had large radar-guided Sparrow missiles.

The RAF adopted the Gloster Javelin, burdened by a wing of over 86m² (926 sq ft) area, which entered service in 1956 with four 30mm cannon and later carried four Firestreak missiles which homed on the heat radiated by the engines of hostile aircraft. Canada built a series of Avro CF-100 long-range interceptors, starting with eight 12.7mm guns and ending with batteries of rockets. France's Sud-Ouest Vautour IIN was heavily armed with four 30mm cannon and 104 rockets. Sweden's Saab J32B combined four 30mm with four Sidewinder guided missiles.

The Soviet Union selected the Yakovlev Yak-25, armed with two 37mm cannon. This was developed into the Yak-27, which was just supersonic, and by 1960 into the Yak-28P which could reach Mach 1.73 when carrying a mix of radar-guided and heat-homing R-8M missiles. Most advanced of the non-starters was the

Republic XF-103, work on which began for the USAF in 1951. Powered by a huge turbojet and ramjet, this 23.5m (77ft) steel aircraft was to fly at 4,180km/h (2,446mph), or Mach 4, at which speed manoeuvres would have been impossible!

*"At the appropriate distance a battery of unguided rockets would be fired 'covering an area of sky as large as a football field'."*

Above: Powered by two SNECMA Atar engines, the French SO.4050 Vautour (vulture) was supersonic in a dive. Like the B-47, the landing gear comprised tandem two-wheel trucks under the fuselage and stabilizing outrigger wheels which retracted into the engine nacelles. This is a Vautour IIN night fighter.

Below: An exceptionally fine aircraft, the Saab J32B was a design dating from 1948-50 yet it still looks modern today. Powered by a Rolls-Royce Avon with afterburner made in Sweden under licence, it could dive faster than sound despite being a heavily armed two-seater with powerful radar.

# US NAVY JETS

The Navy engine firm, Westinghouse, began with turbojets

so small that Grumman had to consider powering the

F9F Panther with four of them!

Fortunately Pratt & Whitney built the British Nene engine under licence, enabling the first F9F Panther to fly on 24 November 1947 with a single engine. The F9F was most successful, and altogether 3,367 were built, the final 1,985 being swept-wing Cougars. Except for dual trainer versions all had four 20mm cannon.

Similar armament was fitted to the McDonnell F2H Banshee, which was powered by two slim Westinghouse J34 engines buried inside the roots of the wing. Unlike the F9F the F2H was

developed with high-power interception radar, and later versions carried up to four of the simple Navy-developed Sidewinder missiles. The Banshee's landing gear, flaps and folding wing were all powered electrically.

McDonnell next built the F3H Demon, with swept wings and tail. This would have been a real winner, but the Westinghouse J40 engine proved a failure. Years late, the F3H-2 entered service in 1956, powered by an Allison J71 engine which, with afterburner boosting thrust, was rated

*"Douglas achieved complete success with the F4D Skyray, which had a huge wing and no horizontal tail."*

Below: Still proudly wearing its Marine Corps 'Midnight blue' livery, this Grumman F9F-4 was typical of hundreds of Panthers which saw action in the Korean war of 1950-53. Like many jet fighters of this era it had permanently fixed fuel tanks on the wingtips. Armament was four 20mm cannon in the nose.

at 6,464kg (14,250lb). Later Demons had radar and either Sidewinders or large Sparrow radar-guided missiles.

Many designers thought jet propulsion called for radically new aircraft shapes. Douglas achieved complete success with the F4D Skyray, which had a huge wing and no horizontal tail. After failure of the planned J40 engine the Skyray entered service with the Pratt & Whitney J57, rated with afterburner at 7,257kg (16,000lb), which enabled these agile aircraft to climb at a rate of 5,300m (18,000ft)/min. Armament was four 20mm cannon.

Even stranger was the Vought F7U Cutlass. First flown in September 1948 on the 3,810kg (8,400lb) combined thrust of two Westinghouse J34 engines, this had a broad swept wing on which were mounted twin fins and rudders, there being no horizontal tail. In June 1954 the F7U-3 entered service with two 2,722kg (6,000lb) Westinghouse J46 engines and armed with four 20mm cannon and four Sparrow missiles.

*Above: This McDonnell F-3B (formerly F3H-2) Demon bears the markings of squadron VF-13, embarked aboard the carrier USS Shangri La. Armament was again four 20mm cannon, later augmented by Sparrow missiles, and an inflight refuelling probe can be seen alongside the cockpit. This version of the Demon first flew in June 1955. Production ceased in 1959, and the last examples were withdrawn from combat duty in 1965.*

*Below: The Douglas F4D-1 (later redesignated F-6A) Skyray appeared to be a tailless delta but actually had a short-span swept wing. Armament was again four 20mm cannon, but unlike the Panther and Demon the guns were in the outer wings. The XF4D prototype flew in January 1951, but failure of the J40 engine delayed squadron service until 1956. Douglas's El Segundo factory delivered 420. They proved effective in service, being popularly called 'the Ford', from F4D.*

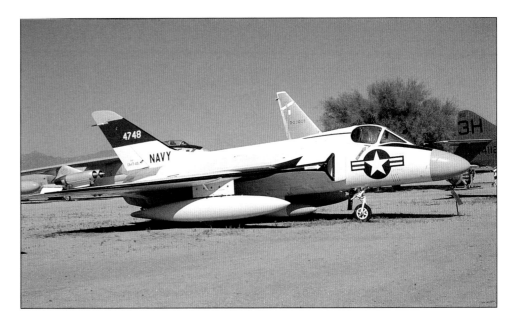

# EUROPEAN NAVY JETS

No European country could afford the enormous carriers of
the US Navy, yet the British inventions of the angled deck and
steam catapult enabled fast jets to operate from quite
modest ships.

Sadly, the British procurement machine was so relaxed after World War II that the Fleet Air Arm had no swept-wing aircraft until 1958.

Even the simple Supermarine Attacker did not enter service until 1951. The Spiteful was a Spitfire with a new laminar-flow wing, and the Attacker was a Spiteful with the Griffon piston engine replaced by a Nene turbojet. Speed was 949km/h (590mph) with four 20mm guns in the wings, and external loads could include bombs, rockets and a large belly tank. The Hawker Sea Hawk was unique in that its Nene engine had the jetpipe bifurcated to a nozzle in each wing trailing edge to enable a fuel

tank to be fitted in the rear fuselage. Otherwise it was in the same class as the Attacker.

The de Havilland Sea Venom culminated in the radar-equipped FAW.22 with side-by-side seats, four 20mm guns and Firestreak guided missiles. After long delays the D.H.110, flown in 1951, reached the Fleet Air Arm as the Sea Vixen in July 1959. Powered by two 5,100kg (11,250lb) thrust Rolls-Royce Avons, the Vixen carried its tail on twin booms which in the FAW.2 version were extended forward to carry extra fuel. Supersonic in a dive, the Vixen could carry guns, rockets, bombs and either Firestreak or Red Top missiles.

*"Supersonic in a dive, the Vixen could carry guns, rockets, bombs and either Firestreak or Red Top missiles."*

Similar engines powered the Supermarine Scimitar, which reached the squadrons 13 years after the start of design in 1945! Fitted with powerful blown flaps, the Scimitar reached 1,186km/h (737mph) at sea level, and carried four 30mm guns, Sidewinder missiles, Bullpup attack missiles and many other weapons.

France's *Aéronavale* used a version of Sea Venom called the Aquilon, and went on to operate the Dassault Etendard attack fighter. This was developed into the Super Etendard used by Argentina in the Falklands conflict, armed with Exocet anti-ship missiles.

*Left: Bearing the 'ace of diamonds' insignia of the Fleet Air Arm's No 806 Squadron, this Hawker (Armstrong Whitworth-built) Sea Hawk is the only example surviving in flying condition. The wings power-folded straight upwards. Later versions backed up their four 20mm guns by four 227kg (500lb) bombs or eight rockets. The Sea Hawk was outclassed in an era of swept-wing jets, but it was agile and easy to fly, and 550 were built for the navies of Britain, the Netherlands, Australia, Germany and India. Note the arrester hook projecting behind the tail.*

Above: A fine portrait of a Dassault Super Etendard of the Modernisé type, serving with the French Aéronavale. Basic armament comprises two 30mm guns and various bombs (including an AN52 nuclear weapon) or Exocet cruise missile. The modernized aircraft have upgraded navigation/attack avionics, including a new Anemone radar.

Left: This Sea Vixen FAW.2 is one of few survivors of an impressive and effective carrier-based all-weather fighter family designed by de Havilland, built by Hawker Siddeley and supported by British Aerospace over 40 years. The tail was carried on two booms, and the pilot sat on the left under an offset canopy, with the radar observer in 'the coal hole' to starboard.

# AMERICAN SUPERSONIC FIGHTERS

The first of the 'Century-series' of USAF supersonic fighters,
the North American F-100 was named Super Sabre but was
a totally new design.

It had a sharp-edged nose inlet feeding a J57 rated with afterburner at 7,257kg (16,000lb), low-mounted 'slab' tailplane, belly airbrake and a wing swept at 45° with slats but no flaps. The four 20mm guns were of a new type.

Altogether 2,239 'Huns' were built, later versions being used mainly in the attack role, culminating in the tandem-seat F-100F used in Vietnam as an FAC (Forward Air Control) aircraft. Maximum level speed was about 1,434km/h (891mph).

McDonnell's F-101 Voodoo seemed over-powered with *two* J57 engines!

Most were single-seat fighter-bomber or reconnaissance aircraft, but the F-101B was a radar-equipped two-seater armed with three Falcon missiles, and also able to carry the Genie air/air rocket with a nuclear warhead. Canada replaced its own next-generation CF-105 Arrow by secondhand F-101Bs which served until 1985.

Convair adopted a bold tailless-delta (triangular) layout for the F-102 Delta Dagger single-seat, radar-equipped interceptor. The prototype flew in October 1953 and proved unable to reach Mach 1! Thanks to new aerodynamic knowledge it was

redesigned, with a longer fuselage of 'Coke-bottle' shape, and 875 were then built, armed with Falcon missiles in an internal bay. An afterburning J57 gave a speed of Mach 1.25 (1,328km/h, 825mph). The pilot had a second control column to control the sweep and range

*Below: Marketed by Lockheed as 'the missile with a man in it', the F-104 Starfighter had a tiny wing and a powerful General Electric J79 engine to thrust it to Mach 2. The marketing was so successful that, though it was limited in capability and unforgiving of the slightest pilot error, nearly 2,600 were built for 16 air forces. This is an F-104G of West Germany's Luftwaffe.*

Above: The Convair F-102 Delta Dagger was originally unable to fly faster than sound. Carefully redesigned with a different fuselage shape it went beyond Mach 1 without difficulty. An unusual feature was that, as seen here, it could fire up to three Hughes Falcon guided missiles from an internal weapon bay.

*"The prototype flew in October 1953 and proved unable to reach Mach 1"*

gates of the radar, and later an infra-red sensor was added above the nose.

Shaken by the MiG-15, Lockheed designed the F-104 Starfighter to have Mach-2 performance, even at the expense of manoeuvrability. Thus, most served in the attack and reconnaissance roles. In contrast, the Navy's Vought F8U (F-8) Crusader was a superb all-round aircraft which, with a J57 similar to that of the F-100, and burdened by carrier compatibility, had higher speed (up to 1,979km/h, 1,230mph) and longer range. A unique feature was a pivoted variable-incidence folding wing.

Above: The Vought F8U Crusader was an outstanding fighter with wings which not only folded but also pivoted with variable incidence (here they are set a few degrees negative, as shown by the position of the leading edge relative to the fixed root). Features included a belly airbrake, four 20mm guns in the fuselage sides and (in the side bulge) a flight-refuelling probe. This aircraft served in 1957 with VF-32 aboard USS Saratoga.

# EUROPEAN SUPERSONIC FIGHTERS

After World War II S.A. Lavochkin's fighters all failed to win
production orders, yet in March 1951 his La-190 was the first
in the world to exceed Mach 1 on the level.

The first European type in service was the MiG-19, operational from March 1955. Features included a mid wing with large flaps and outboard ailerons despite being swept at 60°, and two afterburning AM-9B turbojets each rated at 3,250kg (7,165lb). Fitted with three 23mm cannon, speed at high altitude was 1,454km/h (903mph), Mach 1.367. The MiG-19S introduced a 'slab' horizontal tail, and the MiG-19P radar and four missiles.

The first West European supersonic fighter was the Dassault Super Mystère B2, powered by a SNECMA Atar rated with afterburner at 4,460kg (9,833lb). Armament comprised two 30mm cannon and bombs, rockets or Sidewinder missiles, and speed at high altitude was 1,189km/h (739mph) or Mach 1.12.

Sweden achieved brilliant success with the Saab J35 Draken, powered by a licence-built Avon rated with

*"Though limited in range and endurance, the Lightning was a brilliant aerobatic performer."*

*Below: Seen accompanied by a Dassault Mystère IV, this camouflaged SMB2 (Super Mystère B2) was the first type of West European supersonic fighter in service. This example served with Escadre de Chasse 12 at Cambrai until this unit was re-equipped with the Mirage IIIC in 1962.*

afterburner at 8,000kg (17,635lb) in the final J35F version. Behind the side air inlets the inner wings were swept at an amazing 80°. The outer wings had a leading-edge angle of 57°, and on the trailing edges were four elevons. Early versions had two 30mm guns and later models various missiles.

Britain's Lightning, designed by English Electric and made by BAC and then BAe, had two Draken-type engines one above the other, fed by a fixed nose inlet with a simple radar in the central cone. The wing was swept at 60° but untapered, with ailerons across the tips. The outer wings were filled by the outward-retracting main landing gears, so there was almost nowhere to put fuel until various sizes of belly blister tank were added. Early versions had two 30mm guns and later marks two Firestreak or Red Top missiles. Though limited in range and endurance, the Lightning was a brilliant aerobatic performer.

*Above: Having a unique 'double delta' configuration, in which the fuel and equipment was mainly housed in compartments one behind the other in the long-chord inboard wing, the Saab Draken achieved Mach 2 on precisely half the power of a Lightning. This J35F 'Filip', serving with Wing F10, has six of its 11 pylons occupied by drop tanks and Sidewinder missiles.*

*Below: Few aircraft have ever earned such a large and enthusiastic following of fans as the Lightning. Designed at a time when nobody knew how a supersonic aircraft should be shaped, it was also popular with its pilots. This well-worn F.1 version served with the Wattisham Target Facilities Flight, possibly with inert Firestreak missiles.*

# STAND-OFF KILLERS

Development of guided missiles increasingly put the burden of interception on the missile rather than the aircraft that launched it.

In 1959 the US Navy ordered the Douglas F6D Missileer with a speed of only 879km/h (546mph) but a powerful radar and six missiles with a range exceeding 161km (100 miles). Studies were even made of 'fighters' based on large jet airliners, able to launch as many as 96 guided missiles at incoming enemies!

Like the F-101B the Convair F-106 could launch the nuclear Genie rocket which could destroy a whole enemy formation. The F-106 was a reshaped F-102 with the J75 rated at 11,113kg (24,500lb) with afterburner, giving a speed of 2,454km/h (1,525mph), Mach

2.3. The Lockheed YF-12A, the fastest fighter ever flown at 3,661km/h (2,275mph) was never put into service, and in 1959 two huge tailless-delta interceptors, the North American F-108 Rapier and Avro Canada CF-105 Arrow, were cancelled at a time when some people wondered if Britain was right to think all fighters were obsolete.

No such thoughts bothered the Soviet Union, which toiled ceaselessly to build interceptors able to guard its 33,000km (20,500-mile) frontier. The Yak-28P was replaced locally by the twin-engined Sukhoi Su-15, with a speed of 2,230km/h (1,386mph) and

*"The Soviet Union toiled ceaselessly to build interceptors able to guard its frontier."*

*Below: The Convair F-106 Delta Dart was a direct development of the F-102, but unlike its predecessor it had no difficulty in flying faster than sound. In fact, thanks to being properly shaped, and having efficient air inlets feeding the more powerful J75 engine, it exceeded twice that speed. Armament comprised two nuclear-warhead Genie rockets and four Falcon guided missiles carried internally, plus (from 1973) a 20mm gun.*

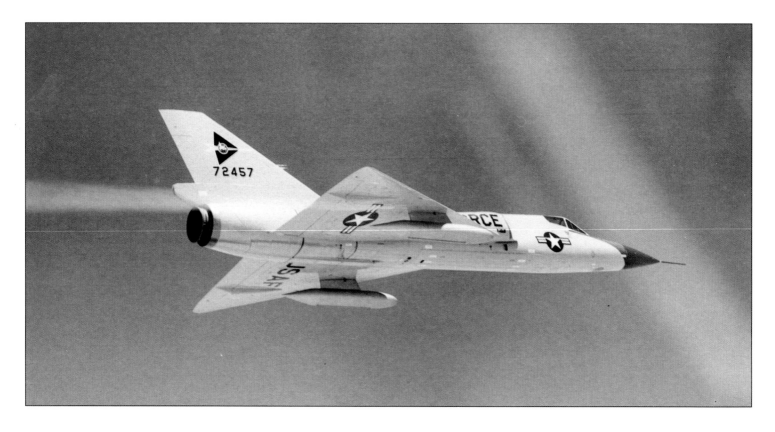

*Right: To defend its vast land area Canada once had a powerful aircraft industry, which in the 1950s delivered 692 CF-100 all-weather interceptors. Developed by Avro Canada, and powered by two locally produced Orenda turbojets, these large two-seaters had exceptional range and endurance. Here an early prototype is testing the wingtip pods planned for the Mk 4 version, firing 60 folding-fin 2.75in rockets. The Mk 4 versions all had a bluff nose housing a large radar, and the Mk 5 had extended-span wings carrying larger pods housing 104 rockets 'to cover an area of sky larger than a football field'.*

*Above: The world's most powerful fighters are the MiG-31 and MiG-31M all-weather interceptors designed in Moscow and made at Gor'kiy (now Nizhny Novgorod). To defend the world's largest country, these have 40 tonnes of engine thrust, and enormous fuel capacity, radar performance and missile power. Here a MiG-31 is being prepared for demonstrations in the West.*

*Right: Today a generation of warplane buffs has grown up who may never have heard of the Gloster Javelin. Distinguished by its broad blunt-tipped wings, large radar operated by a backseater and huge fin carrying a tailplane on top, early Javelins were armed with four 30mm guns in the wings. These are a later version, the FAW.9, with afterburning Armstrong Siddeley Sapphire engines and Firestreak missiles. They were based at Leuchars in Scotland with 25 Sqn.*

missiles able to intercept from 35km (22 miles). For the longest missions Tupolev produced the Tu-128, no less than 30.49m (just over 100ft) long and armed with enormous R-4 missiles with a range of up to 60km (37 miles).

Mikoyan won major contracts with his MiG-25, which in interceptor versions had a speed of 3,000km/h (1,864mph), Mach 2.82, and carried even bigger R-40 missiles with ranges of up to 90km (56 miles). The MiG-25 entered service in 1972. These awesome aircraft were followed by the MiG-31, with two D-30F6 engines each rated at 18,980kg (41,843lb) giving 3,000km/h speed, a service ceiling of 20,600m (67,600ft) and range of up to 3,300km (2,050 miles). Armament includes R-33 missiles with a range up to 125km (78 miles). Mikoyan point out that six could protect the whole United Kingdom.

# MiG-21

Fighter designers studied the fighting between the F-86 and
MiG-15 over Korea. Lockheed then built the F-104 Starfighter,
with a tiny wing, called 'the missile with a man in it'.

In Moscow the MiG bureau insisted on having a wing large enough for superior manoeuvrability – but should it be sharply swept or a triangular delta? After much testing they picked the delta, but retained a horizontal tail. The result led in 1958 to the MiG-21.

Powered by an R-11F-300 rated with afterburner at 5,740kg (12,655lb), this weighed only 6,850kg (15,101lb)

loaded, or less than half as much as typical Western contemporaries. The penalty was that it had just two 30mm guns, and a simple visual radar-ranging gunsight. The plus side was Mach 2 performance and unrivalled dogfight manoeuvrability. This was good enough for many export customers, including India and China which took manufacturing licences.

*Below: Far removed from the agile little fighter schemed by Mikoyan in 1954, this FT7 is a two-seat trainer made by Guizhou corporation in China. Fitted with a Chinese-built version of the original Soviet R-11F-300 afterburning turbojet (itself dating from 1956) the FT7 can exceed Mach 2 on the level and train pupils with a 23mm gun and various bombs, rockets and missiles. This specially painted example is at the Paris Air Show.*

> *"These aircraft have served with 56 air forces, a total which no other fighter is likely ever to equal."*

As early as 1958, prototypes were on test with a larger nose intake incorporating radar. From then on, development continued for almost 20 years, introducing more powerful engines, guided missiles, new guns and extra fuel put wherever room could be found, which was mainly in an enlarged spine fairing from the canopy to the fin. Care was taken never to lose the superb agility and pleasant flight characteristics. As a result just over 10,000 MiG-21s were made in the Soviet Union and approximately 2,000 more in India and China. Even more remarkably, these aircraft have served with 56 air forces, a total which no other fighter is likely ever to equal.

The final versions were designated MiG-21bis. These were powered by the R-25, rated at 7,100kg (15,653lb). Maximum weight is 10,420kg (22,972lb) carrying a twin-barrel 23mm gun, two medium-range missiles or four dogfight missiles, plus a range of attack weapons. Today the Mikoyan bureau and Israel are competing for the potentially huge market fitting new avionics, weapons, instruments and engines to MiG-21 fighters in service around the world.

*Below: In complete contrast, this MiG-21bis is typical of the final production versions, though various upgrades can make individual aircraft even newer. This aircraft bears the post-Warsaw Pact markings of the Hungarian air force. After discussing possible updates for a long time, Hungary has decided to retire its MiG-21s, and is one of several countries actively negotiating involvement in the Swedish Gripen programme (though for reasons of NATO inter-operability the final choice might have to be the F-16).*

# MIRAGE

In 1955 the French company Dassault built a small tailless
delta, the Mirage I. Enlarged prototypes led to the production
Mirage IIIC in 1960.

This version featured primitive radar and an Atar 09B with an afterburning rating of 6,000kg (13,228lb) fed by inlets with half-cone centrebodies which could be screwed in and out according to flight Mach number. An auxiliary rocket engine could be added, in which case the armament was a single air-to-air missile. Without the rocket two 30mm guns could be installed. Despite the obvious limitations, this aircraft (having no competition from Britain) began to find customers all over the world.

The IIIE was fitted with attack avionics, including a doppler navigation radar, and an Atar 9C rated at 6,200kg (13,668lb). For short ranges up to 4,000kg (8,818lb) of weapons could be carried on five pylons, though take-off

*Below: The first-generation Mirages were the Mirage III fighter and the simplified Mirage 5 attack version, which are tailless deltas (the first European fighter to reach Mach 2). These are Mirage IIIE fighter/attack aircraft of the 13th wing based at Colmar near the German frontier. Compared with the original Mirage IIIC they are more powerful, slightly longer and fitted with avionics for low-level attack missions at night or in bad weather.*

was then very long. Again customers were found in many countries, especially after early IIIC fighters performed brilliantly in Israeli hands in the war of 1967. Israel asked for a dedicated visual attack aircraft, trading the radar for more weapons, and the result was the pointed-nose Mirage 5. Total production of these early Mirages amounted to 1,422.

In 1964, via the larger Mirage F2, Dassault produced the Mirage F1 with a conventional wing mounted above the fuselage and a horizontal tail. Powered by an Atar 9K-50 rated at 7,200kg (15,873lb), Dassault delivered 731 to 12 customers.

After trying variable sweep, Dassault returned in the Mirage 2000 to a plain tailless delta, but with powerful slats on the leading edges. The first prototype was flown in March 1978. Powered by a SNECMA M53 rated at 9,687kg (21,355lb), the 2000 is a very different aircraft from the early delta Mirages, though it is also highly priced. It has digital

avionics including much better radar and comprehensive countermeasures (devices to thwart hostile action against the aircraft).

Some versions can carry up to 6,300kg (13,890lb) of weapons on nine pylons, including four kinds of missile. Like some earlier versions, the 2000 can be fitted with a non-retractable inflight-refuelling probe.

*Above: The second-generation Mirage is the Mirage F1 family, with a high-mounted swept wing and a conventional horizontal tail. Among other things this enabled internal fuel capacity to be significantly increased, whilst at the same time reducing the length of runway needed. These two replaced Mirage IIIEs in the 13th wing (see opposite). They have been upgraded to Mirage F1.CT standard, with improved avionics and a non-retractable refuelling probe.*

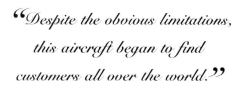

*"Despite the obvious limitations, this aircraft began to find customers all over the world."*

*Left: The third-generation Mirage is the Mirage 2000. Though this marks a return to the tailless delta configuration, it has improved aerodynamics and a more powerful engine. Unlike aircraft of some other countries it is almost Russian in the sheer comprehensiveness of its various avionics and weapon fits. This example, on test at low level before delivery to l'Armée de l'Air, is a Mirage 2000N long-range two-seat bomber. It is seen carrying an ASMP nuclear cruise missile on the centreline, with wing pylons carrying two 2,000-litre (440gal, 528 US gal) drop tanks and two Magic self-defence missiles. An inflight-refuelling probe can be added ahead of the windscreen.*

# PHANTOM

Having lost the first US Navy supersonic fighter orders to
Vought with the F8U, McDonnell designed a formidable attack
aircraft designated AH-1.

By the time the prototype flew in May 1958, it had become the F4H fighter, and in 1962 it became the F-4. Though far from pretty, it was powered by two General Electric J79 engines, each with an afterburning thrust of 7,711kg (17,000lb), fed by fully variable side inlets and with carefully designed auxiliary airflows.

From the start it was clear this aircraft was unbeatable. It had speed up to 2,413km/h (1,499mph), Mach 2.27, tremendous range, a high-power multimode radar managed by a backseater (second crew member), and the ability to carry up to 7,258kg (16,000lb) of external ordnance including virtually every kind of tactical store in the US inventory.

The F-4B entered service with VF-74 in October 1961, going aboard the carrier *Saratoga*. Soon the first of 25 world records was gained – these included absolute speed, climb and sustained altitude – and the demands of Vietnam unexpectedly led to adoption of the aircraft by the USAF. Variants proliferated, though Britain's attempt to improve the Phantom by fitting Rolls-Royce Spey engines actually degraded important aspects of performance.

In the fighter role most versions carried four Sparrow medium-range missiles recessed under the broad fuselage, if necessary supplemented by two pairs of dogfight Sidewinders. Vietnam experience showed difficulty in making sharp manoeuvres at low level whilst carrying heavy bombloads. The lack of a gun was also frustrating in engagements where, for political reasons, the target had to be identified visually. This led to the F-4E, which eventually combined extra internal fuel with a 20mm gun under the nose and a slatted wing.

When production at last stopped (in Japan) in May 1981 total production of this classic aircraft had reached 5,195. Today numerous upgrade programmes are ensuring that some of the dozens of variants will remain operational into the next century.

*Below: One of the 5,000-plus Phantoms was this F-4C, which after service in Vietnam eventually found its way to the Illinois Air National Guard. This version had no internal gun, and the only weapon that can be seen on this aircraft is a Sidewinder missile under the starboard wing. Note that this land-based version nevertheless retained an arrester hook.*

*Right: Taken in 1969, this photograph shows the US Navy's famed aerobatic display team 'The Blue Angels' when they were equipped with the F-4B. In this photograph none of the team are carrying backseaters. This team later re-equipped with the smaller and rather more agile A-4 Skyhawk, and then found their current mount in the F/A-18 Hornet.*

*"From the start it was clear this aircraft was unbeatable."*

*Below: Formating behind the slow photographic aircraft, this Phantom has its leading-edge flaps fully depressed in order to stay airborne. This is an RAF Phantom FGR.2, a totally different variant whose wider inlets fed air to Rolls-Royce Spey turbofan engines. Though much more powerful than the original J79 engines, the installation also greatly increased drag, so that in fact the British Phantoms were slower than the original models!*

# GROUND-ATTACK FIGHTERS

To the popular media, anything that looks like a fighter is
called a fighter, even though it may have no air-to-air
capability. The General Dynamics F-111 was even given
a fighter designation.

Planned to replace the fighter and attack aircraft of the USAF, US Navy and RAF, it combined pivoted 'swing wings' with efficient turbofan engines to give unprecedented range, speed and bombload. With a weight exceeding 45 tonnes (100,000lb) and side-by-side seats it became an excellent bomber and electronic-warfare platform. The only version intended as a fighter, the carrier-based F-111B, failed to meet its performance targets.

Three famous aircraft that look like fighters are the SEPECAT Jaguar, Sukhoi Su-7 and Panavia Tornado. The Jaguar was developed by Britain and France as a light tactical-support aircraft, and emerged as a most useful machine which could if necessary engage other aircraft with two 30mm guns and overwing dogfight missiles. The Sukhoi Su-7 also has two 30mm guns, and was developed into the Su-17 whose pivoted wings enabled bombload to be doubled.

The Tornado was developed by Britain, Germany and Italy as a two-seat multirole aircraft combining Mach-2 speed with a heavy attack load and the latest avionics. Powered by two compact RB.199 afterburning turbofans fitted with reversers to shorten the landing, the Tornado was

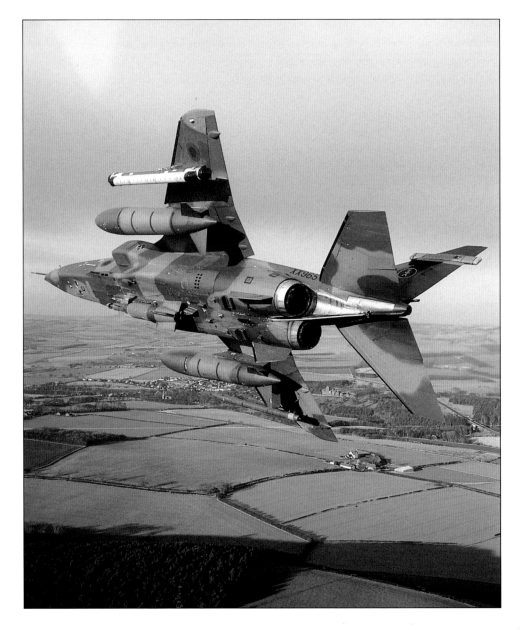

*Right: Originally schemed by the governments of Britain and France as a simple lightweight trainer with limited attack capability, the design engineers turned the Jaguar into a most useful combat aircraft, despite having small Adour engines which even in maximum afterburner give only just over 3,300kg (7,300 lb) thrust each. Jaguars of both the RAF and Armée de l'Air have played a role in many conflicts and peacekeeping forces. This is a Jaguar GR.1 of RAF No 16 Sqn.*

developed into an ADV (Air Defence Version) designed to intercept hostile bombers. Distinguished by its longer and more pointed nose, this can fly at the exceptional speed of 1,480km/h (920mph) at sea level, and at Mach 2.2 at high altitude. Weapons include four Sky Flash medium-range missiles, four Sidewinder or ASRAAM dogfight missiles and a 27mm gun. Like other stand-off killers (p.68) it is not intended for the dogfight kind of air combat.

Sweden's Saab Viggen is noteworthy for its canard (tail-first) layout, giving excellent manoeuvrability and STOL (Short Take-Off and Landing) performance enhanced by a reverser on the powerful Volvo RM8 engine. The JA37 fighter version, first flown in 1977, has a high-velocity 30mm gun and Sky Flash and Sidewinder missiles.

*Above: Seen parked on the original USAF operating base at Tonopah, Nevada, these Lockheed Martin F-117s look weird, like something from another planet. The design of these pioneer 'stealth' aircraft was completely driven by the need to keep its radar cross-section (its appearance on enemy radars) as close to zero as possible. Single-seaters, they have two special engines and carry bombs or missiles internally.*

*Below: Like its predecessor the Draken, the Saab Viggen is a 'double delta', but in this case of a different kind, because there are two separate delta aerofoils in tandem, both fitted with flaps. They enable this Mach-2 aircraft to operate from extremely small rough airstrips. This example is one of the JA37 fighter versions, of which 149 were built out of a total of 329 of all versions. They are currently being upgraded.*

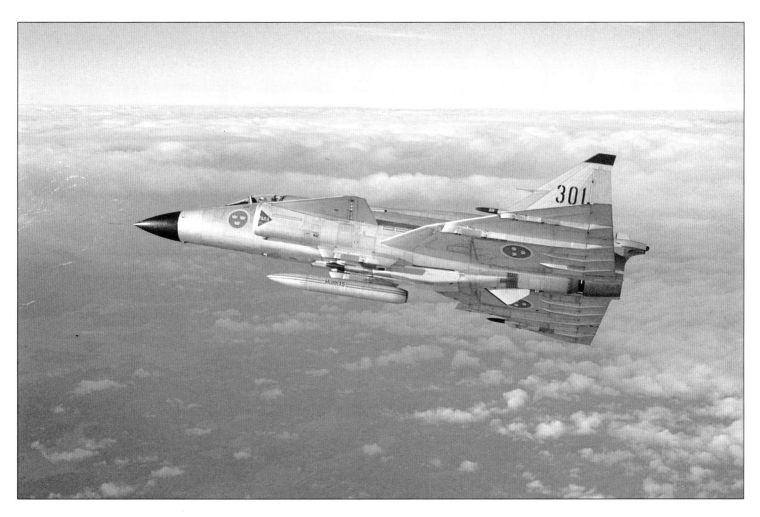

# VERTICAL TAKE-OFF

Around 1960, air forces were worried by the fact that their
costly aircraft were parked in precisely known locations where
any enemy armed with missiles could wipe them off the map.

The result was urgent interest in VTOL (Vertical Take-Off and Landing) aircraft which could disperse into forests or even be hidden in factories or urban buildings.

Today this need has been largely forgotten, and the only aircraft which could be dispersed away from such destruction is the Harrier built by British Aerospace. This is powered by the unique Rolls-Royce Pegasus turbofan, which blasts out through four pivoted nozzles, two for the supersonic fan air and two for the hot core jet. Maximum thrust is up to 10,800kg (23,800lb).

The Harrier is normally operated as a STOVL (Short Take-Off, Vertical Landing) in order to increase weapon/fuel load. The nozzles are pointed backwards for maximum acceleration to liftoff speed. At this point they rotate to 50°, when the lift from the wing plus the vertical component of thrust lifts the aircraft off. The nozzles gradually rotate back to the aft position as the wing takes over. The ship-based Sea Harrier does even better by using an upward-curving 'ski ramp' at the upwind end of the deck of its parent ship.

Land-based Harriers are primarily close-support aircraft, though vectoring the nozzles in flight makes them dangerous air-combat opponents. The Sea Harrier is a dedicated fighter, with radar, two 30mm guns and a mix of medium- and short-range air-to-air missiles. Harriers can also carry up to 6,000kg (13,228lb) of attack weapons.

In the Soviet Union Yakovlev developed the Yak-38 and Yak-38M ship-based multirole fighters with a twin-nozzle main engine and two additional lift jets. The supersonic Yak-141 sadly ran out of money after the collapse of the USSR.

The Harrier will eventually be replaced by a STOVL version of the American Joint Strike Fighter (see pages 94-95). Three main designs are being evaluated, each with different features. All are 'stealth' type designs with vectored main engines in the 15,875kg (35,000lb) class, and the McDonnell Douglas-led design has no vertical tail.

*"Harriers are primarily close-support aircraft, though vectoring the nozzles in flight makes them dangerous air-combat opponents."*

Left: The Harrier GR.5 was an interim RAF version which did at least introduce a larger wing made of carbon-fibre by McDonnell Douglas, which greatly increases fuel capacity and the ability to carry weapons. Today it has been overtaken by the GR.7 with night attack avionics. Both versions can have two 25mm guns and up to 4.9 tonnes (10,800lb) of stores on nine pylons. US Marine Corps Harriers have more powerful engines and can carry 6 tonnes (13,235 lb).

Left: Sea Harrier FRS.1 multirole naval fighters returning to a Royal Navy ship of the Invincible class. Now largely replaced by the radar equipped FRS.2, the original Sea Harrier put up an astonishing performance in the Falklands war, sustaining several combat sorties per day without respite. No other aircraft exists even today which could have flown these missions in the absence of airfields or conventional aircraft carriers.

Below: Taking off from Grottaglie naval air station, this TAV-8B Harrier II of the Italian Navy is typical of the third generation of Harriers. Here being flown solo, the enlarged forward fuselage accommodates the instructor much higher than the pupil to give him the best possible view ahead. Generally similar aircraft are the US Marines TAV-8B and the RAF Harrier T.10.

# F-14 TOMCAT

When in 1968 the overweight F-111B was cancelled,
Grumman – a partner in its development – was well
advanced in studies for a replacement.

The resulting design won a US Navy competition, and the prototype F-14 flew in December 1970. It had slender 'swing wings', fitted with powerful slats and flaps, mounted on top of the two afterburning turbofan engines, which were wide apart and provided the necessary structures on which were mounted the twin fins and slab tailplanes.

Other features included a powerful multimode radar managed by a backseater called a Naval Flight Officer, matched to the 161km (100-miles) range of the Phoenix air-to-air missiles. Other weapons included Sparrow medium-range AAMs and close-range Sidewinders, and a 20mm multi-barrel gun. A very wide range of attack weapons could also be carried, as well as a comprehensive Tactical Air Reconnaissance Pod System filled with electronic sensors. Without Phoenix missiles speed was 2,485km/h (1,544mph), Mach 2.34.

*Right: Here parked in a tight group on the flight deck of USS America, these F-14A Tomcats represent the world's biggest concentration of long-range all-weather interception capability. The overall configuration of the F-14 – adopted after studying dozens of parametric layouts with different arrangements of wing, engines and tail – has proved so good it has been followed by several other fighter constructors, though without pivoted variable-sweep wings. The latter can be 'overswept' to assist parking the aircraft in confined spaces on deck.*

The F-14A was powered by Pratt & Whitney TF30 engines with an after-burning rating of 9,480kg (20,900lb), fed by efficient fully variable inlets under the fixed inner part of each wing. Fuel capacity was a useful 8,951 litres (1,969 Imp gal, 2,365 US gal), augmented by a drop tank and a retractable flight-refuelling probe. Altogether the Tomcat was a worthy member of the Grumman 'cat' family, though prolonged difficulties were encountered with the propulsion system. Eventually the engines were replaced by the General Electric F110,

with a maximum rating of 12,247kg (27,000lb). This not only improved reliability but also enabled the resulting F-14A(Plus) and F-14D to be launched without using afterburner. This has increased mission range by a remarkable 62 per cent, and reduced time to climb to high altitude by 61 per cent.

Over 630 F-14s were delivered, many of the earlier versions being upgraded with new avionics and engines. No aircraft currently planned for the Navy can equal the capability of the F-14/Phoenix combination.

Left: Coming in to land on its carrier the F-14 needs all the lift it can get, with wings spread out to maximum span and with full-span slats, flaps and glove vanes extended. This example is recovering whilst carrying two external fuel tanks, but the Phoenix missile pallets uinder the fuselage are not loaded. Note the exceptionally long vertical reach of the arrester hook.

Below: With the wings at the maximum sweep angle of 68° the F-14 looks like a tailless delta aircraft, because the wings almost merge into the tailplanes. This F-14A, powered by the original TF30 engine, was serving with the Pacific Fleet, and probably photographed over California.

# F-15 EAGLE

USAF studies of the best possible air-combat fighter led to an industry competition, won by McDonnell Douglas with the F-15, first flown on 27 July 1972.

Though the dual-control F-15B was also ordered, the USAF insisted on the design being tailored totally to air superiority, with the slogan 'not a pound for air-to-ground'.

The basis of the design was a broad fixed-geometry wing of 56.5m² (608sq ft), so large that the only movable surfaces are outboard ailerons and plain flaps. The pivoted variable inlets lead to ducts under the wing which curve in to engines mounted close together, so that the twin vertical tails and jagged 'dog-tooth' tailplanes have to be mounted on strong beams along each side. The engines are specially designed Pratt & Whitney F100 afterburning turbofans, each rated at 10,782kg (23,770lb) thrust.

Like the F-14, the multimode radar was provided by Hughes, though that company's Phoenix missile was not adopted. Armament was the traditional mix of Sparrow medium-range and Sidewinder short-range missiles and a 20mm multi-barrel gun mounted in the right wing root, fed from a 940-round drum by a belt passing over the right engine duct. Internal fuel capacity is 7,836 litres (1,724 Imp gal, 2,070 US gal), augmented by a tanker boom socket above the left wing root. Three 2,309 litre (508gal, 610 US gal) drop tanks can be carried, and the F-15C and two-seat D carry conformal tanks scabbed on the flat sides of the fuselage each holding 2,771 litres (609gal, 732 US gal).

*Below: A puff of rubber smoke marks the touchdown point for an F-15C of the USAF 36th Tactical Fighter Wing, then based at Bitburg AB in Germany. The engine air inlets are pivoted downwards, and the huge dorsal airbrake is fully raised to slow the fighter down quickly.*

*"The USAF insisted on the design being tailored totally to air superiority."*

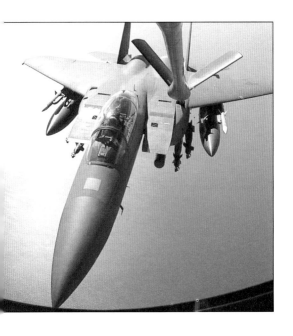

*Left: How a two-seat F-15E Strike Eagle looks to a KC-135 boom operator as the fighter jockeys into position to take fuel over the Adriatic Sea during a peacekeeping mission over Bosnia. Its main offensive load comprises four Paveway LGBs (laser-guided bombs). Outboard of the drop tanks are AMRAAM medium-range radar-guided missiles.*

*Below: Recognisable by its combination of a heavy load of weapons and a two-place cockpit, this F-15E is carrying a load of Mk 82 GP bombs, together with Lantirn guidance pods. Against aerial targets it can use its AIM-120 AMRAAM medium-range missiles and AIM-9M Sidewinder short-range missiles.*

The F-15A entered service in November 1974, since when Israeli aircraft have claimed 56.5 kills, the USAF 36 and the Royal Saudi AF two, without loss. Current production is of the F-15E Strike Eagle which, in a reversal of policy, is a two-seat, dual-role attack fighter with a bomb load of up to 11,113kg (24,500lb). With this load the take-off weight is 36,741kg (81,000lb). Engine options are the P&W F100-229 rated at 13,200kg (29,100lb) or the GE F110. Total production including exports is expected to be 209, on top of 1,222 earlier versions.

# GREAT RUSSIAN FIGHTERS

In parallel with the awesome MiG-25 and MiG-31, the
A.I. Mikoyan team also produced a prolific family of
single-engined 'swing-wing' fighter and attack aircraft
designated as the MiG-23 and MiG-27.

Over 5,800 were built, powered by large afterburning turbojets rated at up to 13,000kg (28,660lb) and able to reach speeds up to 2,500km/h (1,553mph), Mach 2.35.

The emergence of the American F-14 and F-15 naturally spurred development of superior Soviet fighters. Mikoyan's answer was the 9-01 prototype, flown on 6 October 1977. This was refined into the MiG-29, which entered Frontal Aviation service in 1983. It followed the configuration of the F-15, though

*Below: Head-on view of a MiG-33, previously called a MiG-29M, with six of its pylons loaded with two R-27E(R) missiles and four R-73Es. The black dot at the root of the port wing is the aperture for the 30mm gun, and the ball ahead of the windscreen is the combined infra-red and laser unit.*

*Above: Coming in to land this MiG-29 has its wing leading edges fully hinged down, and the engine inlets are still open (on touchdown they will be shut off to avoid foreign-object damage), but the row of auxiliary inlets above the blended wing/fuselage (called the centroplan) are already open.*

*Below: About to land after a breathtaking display, this Su-27PD is based at Zhukovskiy with the 'Test Pilots' team named for legendary pilot Mikhail Gromov. This aircraft has a configuration very much like the MiG-29, though it is larger and more powerful. It has a large airbrake in the same place as that of the F-15.*

*"Most observers would probably agree that, despite its size, the Su-27 is the greatest fighter in service today."*

smaller, with less-powerful engines, more advanced aerodynamics and, surprisingly, better avionics. For 13 years MiG-29 pilots have had the choice of a multimode radar, an infra-red sensor, a laser gun ranger and a helmet-mounted designation sight.

When the German *Luftwaffe* inherited MiG-29s of an early standard when Germany was reunified, they were astonished at the way both the gun and missiles can be used at large off-boresight angles; in other words against targets off to one side or above or below. The GSh-301 in the left wing root is the lightest 30mm gun in the

world, and it generally hits with the first round. Moreover, the choice of air-to-air missiles is unrivalled. Engines are RD-33 afterburning turbofans of 8,770kg (19,335lb) each, and these can have multi-axis thrust vectoring. Among later versions is the MiG-29K for operation from aircraft carriers.

Though based on similar aero-dynamics, Sukhoi's Su-27 is larger and powered by AL-31F engines of 12,500kg (27,557lb) each. Most observers would probably agree that, despite its size – fractionally bigger than the F-15 – the Su-27 is the greatest fighter in service today. It has been developed into a range of improved versions, some having a navigator seated behind or beside the pilot. The AL-35F engines of some versions are rated at 13,560kg (29,895lb), and have circular nozzles able to vector in any direction.

# LIGHT FIGHTERS

In 1955 the Folland Gnat astonished British observers
by its amazing agility. Powered by a 2,134kg (4,705lb) Bristol
Orpheus turbojet, this tiny aircraft was also beautiful.

It stood so low that a man standing on the ground could look into the cockpit through the frameless canopy. Armed with two 30mm guns and bombs, rockets or tanks, the Gnat was adopted by India and developed into the longer-ranged Ajeet which performed well in actual warfare.

Not much larger, Northrop's F-5 Freedom Fighter first flew in July 1959. Powered by two GE J85 turbojets, each with an afterburning thrust of 1,851kg (4,080lb), the F-5 could reach 1,490km/h (925mph), Mach 1.4. Features included a thin unswept wing with missiles or tanks on the tips, two 20mm guns in the upper part of the nose and the ability to carry various attack loads.

This popular aircraft led to the F-5E Tiger II with minor airframe changes, 2,268kg (5,000lb) J85 engines and a wider range of weapons. Altogether Northrop delivered 2,614 F-5s, and a further 776 were made in five customer countries.

One of these countries was Taiwan, which after being refused permission to buy US fighters developed a light fighter of its own. Called Ching-Kuo, built by AIDC, and first flown in May 1989, it looks like a blend of the F-16 and F-18. The two engines are AlliedSignal F125 turbofans each with an afterburning rating of 4,200kg (9,260lb). Apart from the radar and missiles, based on American originals, virtually every item of equipment is imported from the USA, including the 20mm multibarrel gun under the wing on the left side.

*"This totally modern and comprehensively equipped fighter is in full service, and has delighted every pilot who has flown it."*

Clearly the best light fighter today is Sweden's Saab JAS39 Gripen. With an unstable canard layout, it is powered by a Volvo RM12 turbofan with an afterburning rating of 8,210kg (18,100lb). Armament comprises a 27mm gun and a vast range of missiles or other stores carried on seven locations. This totally modern and comprehensively equipped fighter is in full service in single- and two-seat versions, and has delighted every pilot who has flown it.

*Left: Having completed the design of the Canberra, the first British jet bomber, W.E.W. 'Teddy' Petter threw up his job and joined little Folland Aircraft to design the Gnat, the smallest-ever jet fighter. The RAF scorned it but, many years later – fed up with hearing how nice it was to fly – asked Folland to turn it into a trainer, as seen here. To show what the Gnat Trainer was like to fly, it was selected as the first equipment of the Red Arrows, the RAF's premier aerobatic team.*

Right: One of the many customers for the Northrop F-5E Tiger II was the Royal Jordanian Air Force, which today still has more than 50 in service but is eyeing various replacements. This example, with Sidewinder close-range missiles on the wingtips, has its flaps lowered in order to formate with the photo aircraft.

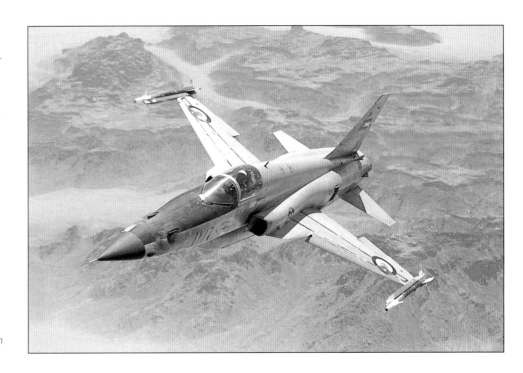

Below: Latest and best of the light fighters is Sweden's Saab Gripen. Though less powerful than most Millennium fighters – it has the same engine as the Hornet but half as many – it is superbly equipped for all air-combat, attack and reconnaissance missions. This example serves with Royal Swedish AF Wing F7.

# F-16 FIGHTING FALCON

When General Dynamics flew the YF-16 on 2 February 1974
it was regarded merely as a demonstrator of LWF
(LightWeight Fighter) technology.

No USAF officer would have dared to damage his career by showing interest; 'Why have a VW when you can have a Cadillac [F-15] ?' They would have been amazed to be told that by 1997 USAF orders for the larger and heavier multirole F-16 would far surpass those for the F-15, and that including 16 export customers the total would nudge 4,000!

From the outset the F-16 was helped by using the same engine, and today choice of engines, as the F-15. It also incorporated later knowledge of unstable design, so that – controlling the trajectory by a small sidestick on the right side of the cockpit, beside the frameless canopy – the pilot can command virtually instant manoeuvres. Instead of having variable sweep the wing has variable aerofoil profile, with automatically commanded leading-edge flaps and trailing-edge flaperons (which combine the functions of flaps

*Below: A fine portrait of an F-16D-40 two-seater of the air force of Bahrain. This customer is one of many to specify the General Electric F110 engine. Initially this superb engine was much more powerful than the Pratt & Whitney F100 fitted to all the first F-16s, but the Connecticut firm have fought back and in their latest F100 versions have engines every bit as powerful and reliable as their competitor. The way the wings are blended into sharp-edged wide parts of the fuselage is taken further in today's Russian fighters.*

*Left: This aircraft, USAF 87-336, is a late-production F-16C Block 30/32 serving with the 23rd Fighter Squadron, 52nd Wing, at Spangdahlem, Germany. It was photographed on anti-radar patrol over Bosnia, with an ASQ-213 defence-suppression pod and AMRAAM and Sidewinder missiles.*

*Below: The view from a tanker about to fire its refuelling boom into an F-16 of the Illinois Air National Guard. The ANG are every bit as skilled and professional as their full-time brethren in the USAF. Illinois used to have two F-16 groups, but now fields only the 183rd, equipped with Block 30 F-16Cs.*

and ailerons). Slab tailplanes control both pitch and roll, all surfaces being commanded by quadruple FBW (fly-by-wire) signals (i.e. electronic rather than mechanical controls).

The F100 or F110 engine is fed by a simple fixed-geometry inlet behind the nose landing gear, and each wing forms an integral tank right to the tip. Just in front of the dorsal fin is a USAF-type flight-refuelling receptacle, and three pylons are plumbed for drop tanks. Weapons include a 20mm multibarrel gun in the blended wing/body fairing on the left side, Sidewinder dogfight missiles on the wingtips and virtually every NATO tactical store on seven other hardpoints. Maximum external load is 5,443kg (12,000lb), and maximum take-off weight of the latest versions is 19,187kg (42,300lb), just double the clean gross weight of the YF-16!

In 1992 GD Fort Worth was bought by Lockheed, and the F-16 is today a product of Lockheed Martin, the biggest defence contractor in the world. They are helping Mitsubishi build the F-2, derived from the F-16 and first flown in 1996. There is every reason to believe that other derived versions of this classic fighter will be in production in 2020.

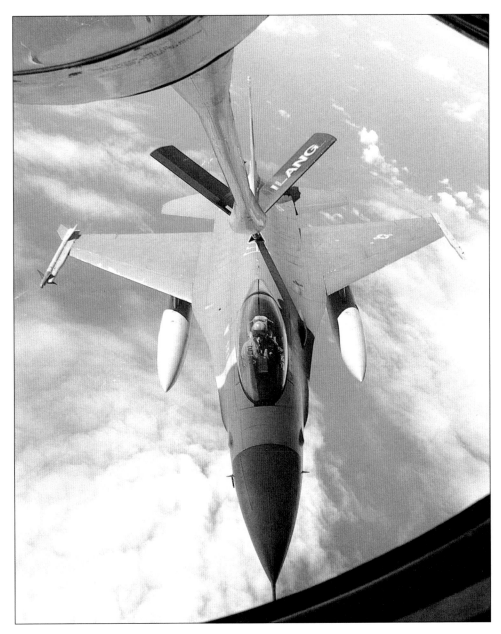

# F-18 HORNET

In 1974 Northrop flew two YF-17 twin-jet lightweight fighters
in competition with the YF-16. McDonnell Douglas teamed
with Northrop to develop these into the F/A-18 Hornet
for the US Navy.

Apart from fitting folding wings, a hook and a twin-wheel nose gear stressed for catapult launch, the naval aircraft was slightly larger, had more powerful engines and much greater internal fuel capacity of 6,060 litres (1,333gal, 1,600 US gal). The prototype flew in November 1978, and the F-18 has since blossomed in many versions which have sold to seven air forces which have no aircraft carriers!

The unswept wing has auto-matically scheduled flaps on the leading and trailing edges, the latter acting as flaperons at low speeds to augment the ailerons and tailerons (tailplanes used for both pitch and roll). Twin fins and rudders, canted outwards, are mounted well forward between the wing and tail. Under the sharp edged wing roots are fixed-geometry inlets to the General Electric F404 engines, rated at 7,258kg (16,000lb) each in early aircraft and 7,983kg (17,600lb) from 1992. Maximum speed is about 1,900km/h (1,180mph).

Most are single-seaters, but some are equipped for two pilots, while the US Marine Corps uses the F-18D Night Attack version with a Naval Flight Officer. Armament includes a 20mm multibarrel gun immediately above the radar and up to 7,031kg (15,500lb) of weapons on nine pylons. An inflight-refuelling probe can be extended from the nose.

One of the biggest aircraft programmes in the world at present is that for the F/A-18E and two-seat

Left: Starting a loop in formation with the photographic aircraft, this two-seat F/A-18B was on the strength of VFA-125, which in 1980 hogged the publicity as the first to fly the Hornet. The F/A-18B is equipped for two pilots and is fully combat-capable, fuel capacity being reduced by a mere 6 per cent.

Above: Steam blasts from one of the catapults of USS America as it hurls a Hornet of VFA-86 'Sidewinders' off the deck. The two rudders rotate inwards towards each other to thrust the tail down and rotate the aircraft nose-up to make the wings lift. This cannot be done in flight but it is repeated on landing.

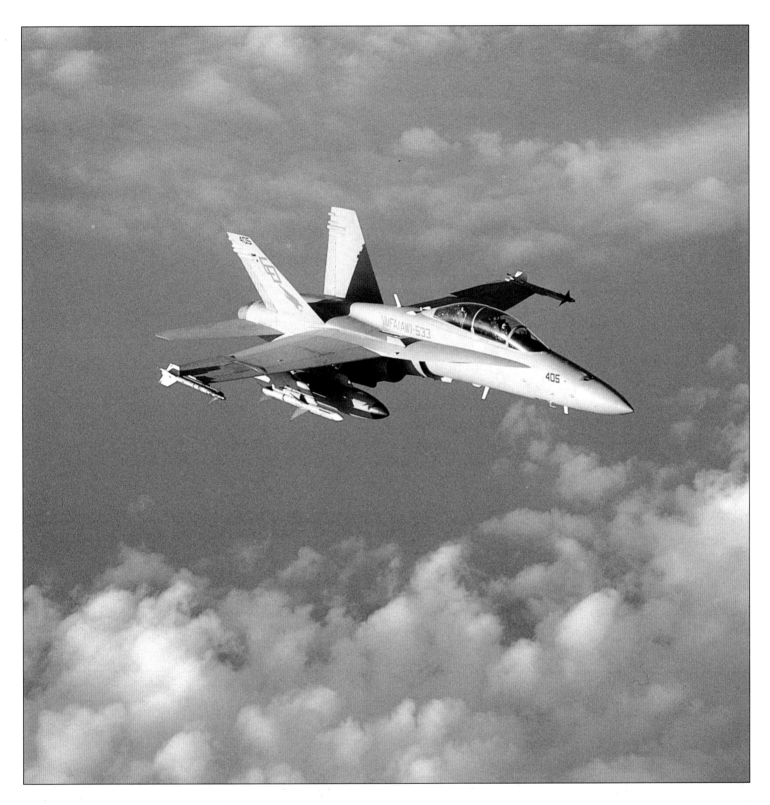

F/A-18F. Powered by F414 turbofans, each with an afterburning rating of 9,979kg (22,000lb), this has a wing enlarged from 37.16m$^2$ (400sq ft) to 46.45m$^2$ (500sq ft), with enormous root extensions under which are the redesigned air inlets. The fuel capacity and weapon loads are significantly increased, without losing air-combat capability. The first F-18E flew in November 1995, and it is planned that the US Navy and Marines will buy 1,000 E/F Hornets by 2015.

*Above: Patrolling off the coast of strife-torn Bosnia, this Hornet serves VMFA(AW)-533, an all-weather squadron of the US Marine Corps equipped with the upgraded F/A-18D two-seater. It is carrying AMRAAMs, Sidewinders and tanks. The photograph was probably taken from an air-refuelling tanker.*

# TOMORROW'S EUROPEAN FIGHTERS

The Soviet Union was a world leader in fighter technology
and its collapse has brought progress almost to a halt.

By mid-1996 Mikoyan had still not succeeded in flying the first prototype of the next-generation 1-42, powered by two SAT-41 engines in the 16-tonne (35,300lb) class.

Even proud France is finding it hard to sustain momentum with the Dassault Rafale. Powered by twin SNECMA M88 turbofans, each with an afterburning rating of 7,439kg (16,400lb) in prototypes, this attractive fighter is in production in three versions, the Rafale B land-based two-seater, the C single-seater and the single-seat M for operation from navy carriers. With the fashionable longitudinally unstable tailless canard delta shape, the Rafale has a 30mm gun and no fewer than 14 attachment points for up to eight tonnes (17,637lb) of external stores, including up to eight Mica air-to-air missiles. Budget pressures have stretched out the production programme, and whittled away at the home market from 336 to about 300.

*"Those who have flown the Eurofighter say it has no equal anywhere in the world."*

*Below: B 01, the first development aircraft for the Dassault Rafale two-seat versions, was ordered in 1989 as a dual-control trainer. It was the first to have RBE2 radar and the Spectra defensive avionics system. In production B versions the backseater will probably be a WSO (weapon-systems officer).*

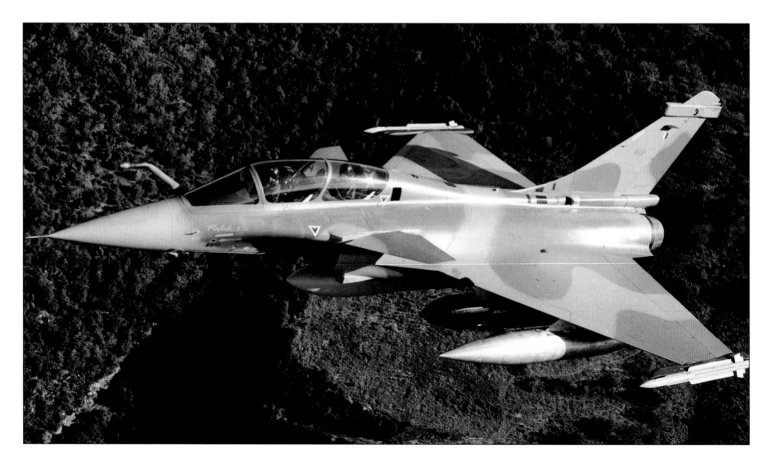

Apart from the very successful Saab Gripen (p.86), the only other European fighter is the Eurofighter. As this is being developed jointly by Britain, Germany, Italy and Spain it has naturally been subjected to terrible political arguments and delays. The only good aspect of this troubled programme is the aircraft itself; those who have flown it say it has no equal anywhere in the world.

Again with unstable canard-delta shape, it is similar in weight to the Rafale, but has a wing of 50m$^2$ (538.2sq ft) compared with 46m$^2$ (495.1sq ft), and twin EJ200 engines each rated at 9,185kg (20,250lb), with planned uprating to 11,930kg (26,300lb). Whereas Rafale has oval side inlets, the multinational fighter has a single variable-geometry rectangular inlet underneath. A 27mm gun is installed on the right side, and up to 6,500kg (14,330lb) of stores can be carried on 13 stations.

*Above: M 01, the first prototype of the single-seat carrier-based Rafale version, first flew in December 1991. It is seen here with Magic dogfight missiles on the wingtips and Mica missiles (infra-red or active radar) under the wings. France is building two large nuclear-powered carriers to project global airpower.*

*Below: Eurofighter DA2 (Development Aircraft No 2) was the last to be powered by the interim RB.199 engine. All the subsequent Eurofighters are fitted with the smaller and more powerful EJ200 engine. Four AMRAAMs are recessed under the broad underside, and Sidewinders under the wingtips, on which are electronic pods.*

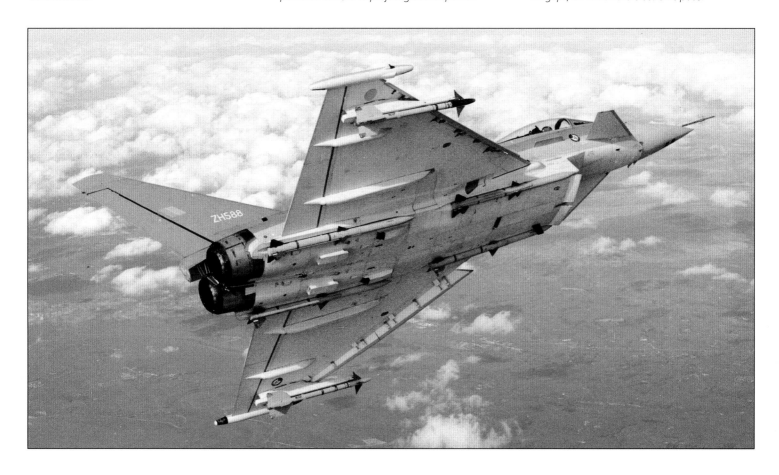

# TOMORROW'S US FIGHTERS

In 1980 the USAF began studying a requirement for 750
(later reduced to 438) totally new Advanced Tactical
Fighters to replace the F-15.

Among the demands were to be low-observables (stealth) technology and supercruise capability (ability to fly at supersonic speed without using afterburner).

From six proposals the USAF picked two for a fly-off contest. In 1990 this began between two Lockheed YF-22s and two Northrop YF-23s, one aircraft of each type being powered by two Pratt & Whitney F119s and the other by the General Electric F120, these being advanced turbofans in the 15,876kg (35,000lb) class. In April 1991 the choice fell on the F-22 with the F119 engine. Lockheed Martin is developing the largely redesigned production F-22A and two-seat F-22B in partnership

with Boeing. Nine development aircraft are to be tested in 1997-2002.

The F-22 is larger than the F-15, with a wing span of 13.56m (44ft 6 in) and wing area of 78m² (840 sq ft), though empty weight (about 14,500kg,

31,970lb) is almost the same. Triplex fly-by-wire signals will control leading-edge flaps, trailing-edge flaperons and ailerons, tailerons and large outward-canted fins and rudders which can operate in opposition as

*Left: Head-on view of the first Lockheed Martin YF-22 prototype, during its rollout ceremony in August 1990 in the United States. The large doors on each side will enclose the main landing gears; unseen here are the double-folding doors under the fuselage which enclose the 4.5m (15ft) internal missile bays.*

*Above: From this angle the YF-22 looks extraordinarily short and stumpy, and the production F-22 will be even shorter (though at nearly 19m, over 62ft, it is nearly as long as a Lancaster heavy bomber). The sloping fins are the same size as the wings of a Spitfire, and wing area is 78m² (840sq ft)!*

*Left: Boeing, which in 1996 purchased losing JSF contender McDonnell Douglas, is building prototypes of this particularly simple 'blended delta' JSF design. Its single engine, with two vectored-thrust nozzles, will be fed by a variable-geometry 'chin' inlet. Boeing has been flying a 94-per-cent scale JSF since 1995.*

*Below: In contrast, Lockheed Martin's JSF has trapezoidal wings and lateral inlets somewhat resembling those of the same company's F-22. In monetary terms JSF is already the biggest fighter programme in history. The USA alone plans to buy nearly 3,000, costing in 1997 money something in excess of $100 billion.*

speed brakes. Diamond-shaped variable inlets set diagonally on the sloping sides of the fuselage will feed the engines which are fitted with variable afterburner nozzles capable of being vectored up or down to improve manoeuvrability. Armament will include a 20mm multibarrel gun and various combinations of missiles in three internal bays. In the attack role up to 2,268kg (5,000lb) can be hung on each of four pylons.

To replace existing tactical aircraft of the USAF, USN, USMC, RAF and RN, the USA and UK are teamed on the JSF (Joint Strike Fighter). The competing airframe contenders are Boeing and Lockheed Martin, and various propulsion systems are being refined by GE, P&W, Allison and Rolls-Royce. All studies so far published show stealth shapes with a single vectored main engine, with or without a nose-mounted lift fan.

# INDEX